Des Wright

Walks in Warwickshire and Worcestershire

Meridian Books

Published 2002 by Meridian Books

© Des Wright 2002

ISBN 1-869922-44-1

A catalogue record for this book is available from the British Library

Maps on pages 10, 15, 19, 23, 28, 32, 36, 41, 45, 50, 55, 61, 66, 70, 75,
81, 85, 90, 94, 98, 103 reproduced from Ordnance Survey mapping on
behalf of The Controller of Her Majesty's Stationery Office © Crown
Copyright. Licence Number MC 100005051

Meridian Books
40 Hadzor Road, Oldbury, West Midlands B68 9LA

Printed in Great Britain by MFP Design & Print, Manchester

Contents

Introduction

How fortunate we walkers are to enjoy such a close acquaintance with the marvellous English countryside, especially with such beautiful counties as Warwickshire and Worcestershire! This third collection of Country Walks explores more of the rights-of-way in those two counties and will, I hope, introduce you to areas through which you have not previously walked.

Maps are needed for our explorations and we must be grateful to our world-renowned Ordnance Survey for the accurate and detailed maps that it provides to help us on our way. The Survey's beginnings were modest. In 1784, the Royal Society, with the support of King George III, commissioned Major-General William Roy, a renowned surveyor, engineer and archaeologist of the time, to lay out, on Hounslow Heath (now part of London Airport), a five-mile-long baseline. From this, the mapping of the whole of Great Britain was ultimately extended using triangulation. However, it was not until 1960 that the OS began to show rights of way on its maps. This method of cartography has now been largely superseded by satellite photography and the quality of our maps is, as ever, second to none. The Pathfinder series, on which are marked details such as field boundaries at the 1:25000 (2½ inches to the mile) scale, has been invaluable to walkers for years. Its worthy successor at the same scale, the Explorer series, has now reached the Midlands and will be complete countrywide by the year 2003.

Some of the field boundaries shown on these maps have disappeared and this sometimes makes it difficult to decide on the precise line of footpaths. Trying to follow a footpath across cropped land may also cause problems. This is especially difficult if the path has not been reinstated, as the law demands, within two weeks of cultivation. So what should we do when confronted with crops growing over the footpaths? Where paths have been reinstated, we stick to them, walking in single file to minimise damage. Where reinstatement has not been attempted, we have to choose one of these options:

- If we are certain about the line of the path, we are entitled to walk through the crop. However, this is sometimes physically impossible (especially through mature maize and oilseed rape) and, after rain, we may be unwilling to get ourselves soaked!

- If we cannot walk through the crop or are reluctant to do so, we have two further choices - to detour round the field margin or to walk along the tracks left by the tyres of tractors which have been used for crop-spraying.

However, we must remember that the relationship between walkers and the countryside is a delicate one. The land on which we walk is the workshop of farmers, market gardeners and foresters and their interests must be respected. Although we walk on rights-of-way, it is our privilege to walk in the countryside and we need to ally that privilege with common sense and by observing the Country Code.

Three questions that have often been asked of me as a result of my first two books are these:

1. 'To which section of the walking community are your books directed?' I obviously try to target a wide spectrum of walkers. On the one hand, I wish to encourage those 'beginners' who are anxious to explore the countryside but who are not yet confident enough to plan their own routes using an OS map. However, I also hope to interest those practitioners who are more experienced and who are looking for new angles and experiences or who might adapt and add to the walks suggested.

2. 'Why did you begin the walk at that particular point?' The answer is that the starting point has to be a compromise between access to public transport and availability of reasonable parking facilities.

3. 'Why didn't you walk the circuit the other way round?' I have tried out the walks each way. Often, the direction is easily decided upon from the viewpoint of scenery. However, occasionally I have found the decision to be more difficult. The walk round Clent and Walton Hills (Walk 1) presented the greatest difficulty, both clockwise and anticlockwise routes providing spectacular views to the south. The final decision – to walk anti-clockwise – was made after a small opinion survey amongst walkers *en route* and to those who took part, my grateful thanks! However, to get double value from this volume, I suggest that, when you have tried each walk in the suggested direction, you go back and walk each one the other way round! You may be surprised how different the scenery looks from the opposite aspect - but don't get lost!

Incidentally, three things plague writers of walking guides:

- Changed road numbers - which can make nonsense of instructions as to where the walks begin.
- Changed pub names - and isn't it a pity to see some of the old names disappearing?
- Diverted paths - whether legal or illegal.

I hope that, if any such changes have occurred since the book was written, they have not confused you too much.

Several people have given me valuable help in the preparation of this book. They include

Andy Bean and Nigel Chapman (information on the Blue Lias Rings walks), British Waterways, Mr R H Davis (Astwood Bank), Robert Goodchild (Knotts Farm, Hanbury), Nicholas Holding (Permission to quote from *Down along Temeside*), Thomas Hunt (Coughton,)Nia Jones and Michael Hall (MAFF, now DEFRA, Helpline - information on oilseed rape and mink), Dave Milton, Christine Oliver (Sambourne), John Partington (Clent), Brian and Rene Phillips (Cookhill Ramblers), Peter Pritchard (Alcester War Memorial Town Hall), Len Quartly (Cookhill Parish Council), Shirley Reading (Author of *Claverdon - A Century of Change*), the late John Whybrow (help with the Feckenham-Bradley Green walk), Fiona Watson (help with photographs) and Jimmy Yuill (help with the Beoley walk and for use of the sketch on page 29). My son Chris has again willingly undertaken the drawing of the maps and I am most grateful to him for his time-consuming and painstaking work. My wife Pauline has helped with route-checking and has been most patient during the long hours that I have spent at the word-processor. Finally, my sincere thanks go to Peter Groves, the publisher of Meridian Books. Peter, a very experienced walker, has checked all the walks himself, and has given me much-valued support and encouragement.

In conclusion, may I offer you Ten Tips?

1. Read through the instructions before you set out - preferably with a Pathfinder or Explorer map in front of you.

2. Be certain that you are starting at the right place - otherwise the instructions that follow will never make sense.

3. Particularly if you are leading a group (and wish to remain popular!), 'recce' the route in advance and, on 'the day', always keep a couple of sentences ahead in the instructions. This way, you are less likely to have to retrace your steps - and those of your party.

4. Assume that pub car parks are for the use of those who intend to patronise the premises. To assume otherwise would be discourteous to the landlord.

5. Be properly equipped. One consequence of our climate is rain and one consequence of rain is mud. So, for most of the year, boots and suitable rainwear are recommended.

6. After wet weather, take great care when crossing stiles and wooden footbridges - they can be very slippery.

7. Remember to carry a pair of secateurs in your rucksack to cut your way through overgrown vegetation around stiles etc. Even though all the walks are along rights-of-way, some of the footpaths are little-used and, in summer and autumn, can become heavily overgrown.

8. When walking along a country lane and hearing a car approaching from behind, do not lurch back onto the roadway as soon as the car has passed - as with Number 11 buses, there's often another one right behind it!

9. If you use walking poles, take great care to avoid impaling the person who is walking directly behind you, especially when you are climbing over stiles.

10. If you take a dog with you, keep it under close control and do not assume that everyone you meet appreciates your dog as much as you do - indeed, some people might even be afraid of or dislike dogs!

I close by quoting a maxim of fellow Institute Rambler, Malcolm Willetts - 'There's no such thing as a bad walk; it's just that some walks are better than others.' I hope that you agree!

Happy walking!

Des Wright,

Kings Heath, Birmingham

Public Transport

Although details were believed to be correct at the time of going to press you should always check times carefully before setting off. Some appropriate telephone numbers are:

British Rail: 0345 484950

Traveline: 0870 608 2608

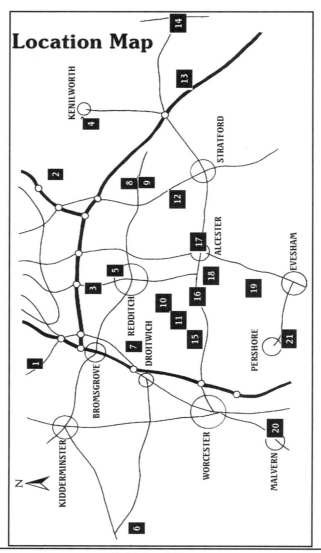

Location Map

KENILWORTH

STRATFORD

ALCESTER

EVESHAM

REDDITCH

DROITWICH

PERSHORE

BROMSGROVE

KIDDERMINSTER

WORCESTER

MALVERN

N

1

Clent and Walton Hills – Contrasting Views

This walk, over two beautiful hills, explores an area where rural Worcestershire nearly meets the West Midlands conurbation.

Distance: 4½ miles.
Start: The Hill Tavern, Clent (GR926798)
Maps: Landranger 139; Pathfinder 953 &933; Explorer 219.
Car Parking: Near the Hill Tavern at the top end of Adam's Hill in Clent.
(GR926798) Adam's Hill leaves the main road through the village at the Fountain Inn.
Public Transport: 1) Bus service 192 Birmingham/
Kidderminster/Ludlow. *Adds 2 miles.* Alight at Hagley Forge and then follow the route shown in the box on page 12.
2) Bus service 100 Barnt Green/Clent/ Kidderminster *Limited service. Sundays and Bank Holidays only.* Alight near The Fountain Inn and walk along the raised path to the side of the road to reach Mount Lane, then read from ★ below.
Refreshments: The Hill Tavern and The Fountain Inn in Clent and at the Nimmings Country Centre (light refreshments).

FROM the Hill Tavern where the walk begins, walk down Adam's Hill and, near the telephone kiosk, fork left into Mount Lane (*192 service bus travellers ending the walk continue along Adam's Hill and return to the instructions in the box on page 12*) at the end of which you reach a road junction. Here turn left.

★ *Bus travellers join here.*

Continue (along Odnall Lane) on a narrow pavement. When the pavement ends, cross the road with care soon to walk beside a sunken stream, the surrounds of which bear luxurious growths of mosses and liverworts which thrive in its humid atmosphere.

This is the Elsie Partington Walk. Elsie Partington's husband John was the head teacher of the local school from 1955 until 1975. Mrs Partington, who became blind in 1975, led a very active life in the village and was often to be seen walking along this path, white stick in hand. She died in 1977. As a memorial to her the Clent W.I. arranged for this path to be so named.

On reaching a crossroads, go straight ahead and, immediately beyond the lych gate of Clent church (which is dedicated to Saint Leonard who is the Patron Saint of prisoners), fork left onto an enclosed path which leads past the graveyard, some parts of which are, in early spring, carpeted with snowdrops. After passing through a kissing gate, continue on a well-used path up a grassy slope through two fields at the top of which you go through another kissing gate. Walk ahead, soon to join a bridleway on which, having passed a National Trust notice, you continue your climb to the trig point at the top of Walton Hill.

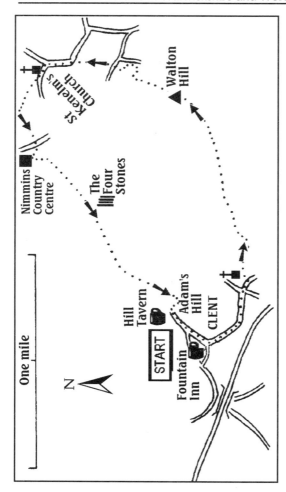

Much of this walk is on land owned and managed by the National Trust. At 1033 feet, Walton Hill tops its neighbour, Clent Hill on your left, by about 36 feet. You will notice that the area is popular for the exercise of four- as well as two-legged animals, some of the more friendly canine visitors being only too willing to share your sandwiches as you use any of the abundant seats with which to enjoy the surrounding views.

From the trig point, walk ahead on the broad bridleway picking out, to your half-right on clear days, Birmingham's BT Tower, the University of Birmingham's Chamberlain Tower and, nearer, Frankley Beeches. When you reach a grassy space surrounded on three sides by wooded slopes, you will see a North Worcestershire Path waymark. Here turn right to join a red-shale path which gently curves its way down the hill. After a little more than 250 yards, look out for a set of seven wooden steps (one up and six down) on your right. Use these to continue down a sharp slope, at the bottom crossing a road to a stile.

The path across the next field can be extremely muddy in winter and, should you prefer to keep excessive mud off your boots, you can avoid it via the following diversion which adds about 650 yards to your walk. (Do not cross the stile ahead of you but turn right onto the road and, immediately, go left. At the next junction, go left again and, at the bottom of Ivy Lane, go left again. When the road swings abruptly right, go with it, rejoining the shorter route at ★ ★ on page 10.

Keeping to the main route, climb over the stile and go half-left down this long field to negotiate, in its far left-hand corner, another stile which leads to a road along which you turn left.

★ ★ Continue on the road down an incline for 100 yards where you turn left into Chapel Lane soon passing interesting patterns in the brickwork in

Chapel Farm which distinguishes the original 1868 building from the extensions of 1988. When you reach the lych gate of St Kenelm's Church, go through it (under a wooden effigy of St Kenelm) and walk down to reach the delightful church the tower of which, built around 1475 and lavishly-ornamented with carvings, seems rather out of proportion to the rest of the building.

St Kenelm's Church, Romsley

Although the church is generally locked, there is much to interest the visitor on its outside, including its Tudor porch (built in the 1550s) in which the Norman doorway is surmounted by a magnificent sandstone tympanum, carved in the middle of the twelfth century, which depicts Christ In Majesty.

With your back to the porch, turn left and walk eastwards looking out, on the south wall high up to the right of the porch, for a small carving of a priest – some say that this represents Saint Kenelm. Pass through a kissing gate to join a path which leads to down Saint Kenelm's Well, but beware of the wooden steps and duckboards which can be very slippery after wet weather.

Legend has it that Kenelm, who in AD819, at the tender age of eight , was King of Mercia, was murdered by supporters of an ambitious and jealous sister and buried on this site. It became a place of pilgrimage, healing powers being attributed to the water from a spring which arose beneath the church's altar – but heed the notices advising you that the water is now unfit for drinking.

Having visited the well, go back up the steps and walk westwards past the church porch on the tarmacked path as it swings right by the tower and then *left* up a gentle slope. After 20 yards, just beyond a metal lamppost, turn right between the yew trees to reach a kissing gate. Now go slightly left to begin the ascent of the second hill on your walk. Guided by a stout, yellow-topped marker post, you reach a stile at the top corner of the second field. Having gone over this, go left and (immediately) right passing another three marker posts. At the third of these, turn sharp left and, after crossing (or walking past) another stile, bear slightly right as you climb up a grassy slope towards coniferous trees.

When you reach a road by these trees, go right and soon left to enter the Nimmings Country Centre where you may be able to buy light refreshments.

From the café, climb up *two* flights of wooden steps and continue up the sharp slope ahead. When you reach the top of the ridge, turn right onto a shale path which leads to the top of Clent Hill.

Since you reached the ridge top, you have walked with mature beeches on your right and their younger successors on your left. You will soon reach a large rock on which is a tablet telling you that the young beeches form Hollis Copse, planted in memory of Jim Hollis, a highly-respected Scout leader from Quinton.

Continue ahead on the ridge path. At the top of the hill you reach the Four Stones and a horizontal toposcope built, and recently refurbished, by the Rotary Clubs of Stourbridge and Kidderminster.

The Four Stones may appear to be the remnants of a prehistoric religious site but this is not the case. They were erected in the mid-eighteenth century by the then Lord Lyttleton of nearby Hagley Hall.

Having visited these features, go back to your path beside the Four Stones and look for a prominent pair of pines surrounded by many other younger ones. Walk to the right of these pines to examine another interesting toposcope, this of the pictorial variety, which was erected by the Automobile Association in 1985.

Leaving this view-identifier on your right, now walk straight on passing a triangular patch of gorse and soon joining a wide downward-sloping bridleway from which you may enjoy, on clear days, breath-taking views across a wide panorama of Worcestershire, Shropshire and far beyond. Ignoring side branches, stay on the main track until it twists abruptly to the right. A few yards after this, go *sharply* right onto a path from which you will soon see the Hill Tavern, your starting point, below you.

Bus travellers continue reading from the start.

Bus travellers (Service 192)

From Hagley Forge Garage walk along Bromsgrove Road (left of the garage). Take the first left (Hall Lane, opposite the Lyttleton Arms) and then, reaching the entrance to Hagley Hall take the signed footpath on the right. Note here the 1914 drinking fountain.

Follow the enclosed path, soon passing Hagley Hall on the left. Pass through a metal barrier and continue forward, soon to go through a squeeze stile. Follow the enclosed path, cross a track and go forward between metal fences. Cross a driveway and reach a road, turning left along this. Reaching a crossroads continue forward (signed Walton Pool, Romsley). Pass the Fountain Inn and walk along a raised path to the side of the road, soon joining the main walk as it comes in from Mount Lane. Now read from ★ on page 9.

To return to the bus: Continue down Adam's Hill and on reaching Odnall Lane turn right. At the road junction continue forward along Woodman Lane and turn right along the path signed to Hagley. Cross a drive and continue forward. At the cross-paths go through the squeeze stile and back along the path to reach the road. Turn left along this, then right along Bromsgrove Road to return to Hagley Forge Garage.

2

Temple Balsall, Balsall Common and a Windmill

This is an ideal walk for those who prefer to walk 'on the flat'!

Distance: 7 miles (*rail travellers only*) or 8½ miles.
Start: Lady Katherine Leveson School, Temple Balsall (GR208761).
Maps: Landranger 139; Pathfinder 955; Explorer 221.
Car Parking: A car park 'for the convenience of visitors to Temple Balsall' is opposite the Lady Katherine Leveson School on Fen End Road West, Temple Balsall near its junction with the B4101. (GR208761).
Public Transport: Bus service 197 from Solihull stops at Temple Balsall near Fen End Road West. Some trains on the Birmingham to Coventry line stop at Berkswell. Leave the station on its south side (cross the bridge if arriving from Birmingham) and walk along the road to reach The Railway Inn. Now start reading from ★ on page 16.
Refreshments: Ye Olde Saracens Head and The Shay House (Balsall Common) and The Railway Inn(Berkswell).

Starting outside the school, walk away from the road junction initially using the pavement. Continue, with care, on the right-hand side of this busy road for about 300 yards until, just before reaching the back of the Temple Balsall village sign, you turn left onto a signposted path and proceed with the hedge on your left. On reaching the end of this large field, cross the stile ahead of you (NOT the one on your left). ★ ★ Walk forward, on the Heart of England Way, with a hedge on your right.

Due to changing agricultural practices, the number of skylarks is reducing quickly in Britain. However, in this area in spring and summer you may be fortunate to hear 'larks carolling from on high in the heavens', to quote the words of that genuine countryman, Phil Drabble.

After the next stile, which is a few paces from the field's corner, a well-trodden path leads you ahead across the field to a hedge-end. Walk on (the hedge on your right), go ahead when the hedge peters out and, after crossing another stile, go very slightly left across a meadow to cross a stream by way of a footbridge.

When you have done this, walk up the slope, aiming for a hedge elbow some 50 yards to the left of the black-and-white gable-end of the picturesque and appropriately-named Magpie Farm. On reaching the hedge, continue alongside it and an overgrown pool to a stile in the corner. Go over this stile into Magpie Lane and turn left. In 75 yards, opposite a green barn, take the path on your right and continue across rough ground. When you approach houses, the path swings left and then right to reach a lane. Here turn left soon to reach the busy Balsall Street. Turn right and walk in front of Ye Olde Saracens Head.

There is a gruesome connection between Temple Balsall and the name of this pub. The manor of Balsall was given to the Knights Templar in the thirteenth century and they built a church there. The Knights Templar protected

Saracens Head inn sign

Crusaders who flocked to the Holy Land from their enemies, amongst whom were the Saracens. The pub sign depicts one of those Saracens.

Just beyond the pub, cross the road with care to negotiate the stile alongside Elm Cottage. Walk on, hugging the left-hand margin of the field, following the path as it swings right by farm buildings and then left. After the next stile, go straight ahead, soon crossing a stream via a plank bridge. Having ascended a slight incline and crossed another stile, continue ahead with hedge and barbed wire on your left.

During World War II, the duty of the War Agricultural Executive Committees was to ensure that all farmers made the most of the land they farmed. Frances Mountford, in her splendid book Heartbreak Farm, *tells of the eviction of her father, with little notice and no compensation, from his farm near Lichfield by officials of the 'War Ags.' Apparently, a similar fate befell Mr R E Phelps of Grange Farm, Balsall Common, the farm which is now to your right.*

At the end of the field, pass through a large hedge gap, negotiate an area which can be muddy in winter and then turn left to cross a stile under an oak tree. Walk ahead for a little over 100 yards with a hedge on the left and, at the end of the field, turn right and then continue, a hedge still on your left. When, after about 300 yards, the clear path veers off, half-right, follow it, cross a stile and the plank bridge beyond it and then continue straight across a meadow to reach a lane. Turn right onto this and walk on for 150 yards or so and, shortly after the lane bends to the left, take an enclosed path on your left which eventually leads to another busy road by The Shay House.

Walk on past the pub for a few yards and cross the road by using a refuge just before the roundabout. On reaching the other side, turn left and walk ahead on the pavement of Hallmeadow Road until you reach another roundabout. Here you turn left (signed Berkswell village) and, with care, walk across a narrow, high-walled railway bridge and continue for a little over 150 yards

Just beyond the half-timbered barn of Lavender Hall Farm, turn right and climb a steep bank to join a path which initially leads through a haulage yard and then continues with the footbridge of Berkswell station soon coming into view straight ahead. The path gradually slopes down and, after a couple of hundred yards and just before tall evergreens, you cross a plank bridge and a double stile on the left to enter a field.

Now continue on your original heading for a further 250 yards when you should look out for a stile on your right. Cross this, walk between fishing pools, pass to the right of the fishery offices and then cross the railway by another bridge at the top of the slope ahead of you. Having done this, turn left and walk parallel to the railway track. After a stile, you veer slightly right over waste

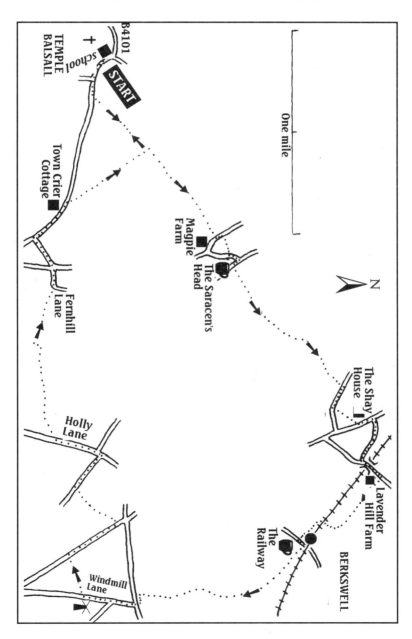

ground to emerge onto a rough lane. This leads to a road near to The Railway Inn, Berkswell, which boasts bars with parliamentary names.

★   *Rail travellers join and leave the walk here.*

Cross the road to climb a stile which is opposite the pub, alongside the entrance to the station car park. Walk ahead using three more stiles, all of which are beside gates which you may find conveniently propped open! After the third stile, keep close to the hedge on your right for about 100 yards when you cross a stile and turn left to follow the path, now with the hedge at your left hand.

From time to time, there are large numbers of rabbits in this area. However, rabbit populations fluctuate violently, sometimes through myxomatosis and sometimes through drastic human intervention.

After crossing a double stile surrounding a plank bridge, walk on the right of barbed wire until, after the next stile and plank bridge, you go half right to pass over a stile beside a gateway. Beyond this, your path hugs the hedge on your left. After yet another stile and plank bridge, aim just to the left of a pair of large greenhouses. When you reach a pair of stiles, cross the one in front of you (NOT the one on your left) and go ahead, to the right of the greenhouses, to cross another stile. Here turn right along an enclosed path going through a wicket gate to reach a road. Turn left along this and soon right into Windmill Lane. Just before Hob Lane, you hear the garrulous voices of a wide range of breeds of chickens, ducks and geese. Walk on along Windmill Lane soon to reach the photogenic Berkswell windmill.

This brick-built windmill, built in 1826 and with its internal machinery still intact is most picturesque, particularly in bright sunlight.

On the opposite side of the road, 25 yards beyond the windmill, join an enclosed path which leads to a stile beside a gate. Cross this (or go through the gate if the stile is obstructed) and walk beside a wall passing stables on the left and into a field, the right-hand boundary of which you

The Berkswell windmill

follow to reach an busy road. Carefully cross the road and turn right onto a sunken pavement. A few paces before the *first* green road sign, turn left onto a tarmacked lane leading to an 'entertainment venue' and an equestrian centre. Shortly after this veers to the right, cross a stile on your right and walk behind wooden stables and continue with wooden palings on your left.

On reaching a pair of farm gates, go through the one on the *right*. Immediately turn left soon to pass a red-brick cottage with a corrugated iron shed attached to it. Pass through a gateway just beyond the cottage and continue over a metal stile to walk through rough ground to emerge, via another metal stile, onto a lane where you turn right. When the lane joins a road (Holly Lane), turn left and stay on this road for about 400 yards when you turn right immediately beyond the metal railings of a small bridge. Walk on, close to a stream, for about 100 yards.

When the stream veers off slightly to the right, go half-left to climb a stile on the other side of the field. Turn right and continue, hedge on your right, to cross a plank bridge plus stile. Your right-of-way goes half-left across the next field to its far left-hand corner. Pass through a gateway and proceed with the hedge at your left hand for 200 yards where you turn left and in a few yards pass over a stile. Beyond it, immediately turn right and follow the hedge to cross another stile at the end of the first field. Your next stile is 35 yards to the left of the second field's corner. Having climbed over this, walk with a fence and hedge on your right to another beyond which is a lane (Fernhill Lane). Turn left into the lane and continue on it, through the crossroads, until you reach a road junction with a Victorian post-box on a corner. Turn right and, in 400 yards, the road swings left.

On the left-hand corner stands the fascinatingly-named Town Crier Cottage – so-called not because of a Town Crier but in memory of a racehorse of that name which was stabled here.

Here be alert at this road bend for, immediately after the first driveway on the right (leading to Gate Farm), you must enter an enclosed path which is easily missed. You thus re-join the Heart of England Way. Having emerged from the enclosed path into open fields, continue (with hedges on your right) until reaching the end of the third field.

Now turn left to walk with a hedge on the right, so rejoining your outward route. (Rail travellers, should they choose not to visit Temple Balsall, should cross the stile on their right and follow the text from ★ ★ on page 13)

Walk ahead to reach Fen End Road into which you turn right for the last leg of your walk. Just before the school, turn left to explore the beautiful Church of St Mary the Virgin with rows of grotesques looking down on you from their lofty perches around the sandstone building. On your way back to the car park, you may be able, on summer afternoons, to take tea in the seventeenth century almshouses.

Rail travellers who have diverted to Temple Balsall now continue from the start on page 13.

3

Another Circuit from Alvechurch

A gentle stroll from a pretty village within easy reach of Birmingham.

Distance: 4 miles or 6 miles. N.B. for those starting and ending at
Alvechurch Station, each of the walks is one mile shorter.
Start: The Square, Alvechurch (GR028726)
Maps: Landranger 139; Pathfinder 953 and 954; Explorer 219/220.
Car Parking: There is a free car park off Tanyard Lane which branches
off Red Lion Street by the Red Lion public house just north of The
Square in Alvechurch. From the car park, walk back via the path
alongside the Red Lion to the Birmingham-Redditch road and turn right
to reach the Square where the walk starts.
Public Transport: Midland Red bus service number 146 connecting
Birmingham and Evesham serves Alvechurch. Trains on the Cross-City
Rail line from Lichfield to Redditch stop at Alvechurch. If using the train
turn right on leaving the platform, join the walk at ★ below and leave it
at the station on the return leg.
Refreshments: The Red Lion and the Swan, both in Alvechurch, and
the Crown Inn at Withybed Green.

ROM The Square cross the Birmingham to Redditch road and walk up
Bear Hill for about 70 yards. When you reach the Memorial Green (which
was formerly the parish pound in which stray animals were held until they
were claimed), fork left up a tarmacked drive which leads you into the
churchyard of St Laurence's Church. Walk past the left (south) side of the
church, maybe exchanging stares with its four fine grotesques as you go.
Continue through gates at the churchyard's west end and along School Lane
ahead, at its end crossing Station Road. On the pavement opposite, turn left
and walk on for a little over 100 yards where you cross the road again to enter,
just before the first of a line of houses, an enclosed path which soon decants
you into the station car park. Go straight ahead across this.

★ *Rail travellers join the walk here.*

Pass through a wire-covered metal gate at the left-hand end of the platform,
ignoring a waymark pointing along the side of the railway. Then, having
'stopped, looked and listened' to check that the line is clear, cross the railway
track with great care. At the other side, climb the staircase at the top of which
you turn sharply left. After a few yards, your path swings right and, after a stile,
follows a clear route half-left across a field to reach a tall hedgerow and brook,
on the right of which you continue ahead. At a giant oak, veer left and pass
under the canal bridge (and mind your head!).

*Opened in 1815, the commercial viability of the Worcester and
Birmingham Canal was soon to be drastically affected by the opening of the
railways in the 1840s. Despite the 58 locks in its 30 miles between Birmingham
Gas Street and Worcester, it is now heavily used by pleasure craft.*

You now begin a gentle ascent which will last for nearly three-quarters of a
mile. You first climb steps to a redundant stile at which you turn right keeping

the hedge and trees of Scarfields Dingle on your right. When these veer off sharply to the right, you bear slightly right and continue your ascent, always staying within about 25 yards of the boundary hedge/fence. After about 350 yards, you reach a metal cattle trough near houses. Here cross a stile on your right then bear left to continue on your original heading. Immediately pass to the right of a tree-fringed pit and walk on, with the hedge at your left until, just before a well-proportioned oak on the skyline, you cross a stile into a lane. Turn right and walk on, possibly enjoying good views to your left beyond Redditch into the distance. When you reach a T-junction, you have reached the summit and deserve a breather.

You will see, on your right, a concrete trig point (193 metres or 633 feet) and also a comparison of modern technology (an elaborate mobile phone aerial) with that of bygone days (a fallen, metal wind-pump).

When you are refreshed, continue ahead down Stoney Lane (the wide grass verge on its right side being a useful refuge if there is traffic) with good views ahead, on clear days, of the slender spire of Tardebigge Church set against the backcloth of the Malverns. At the bottom of the hill, the road narrows and becomes less hospitable to walkers so you will need to proceed cautiously in single file, especially as the highway swings to the right. Immediately beyond the half-timbered Cattespool House, turn right onto a bridleway (signed Cattespoole Mill) and proceed on a concrete driveway.

Shortly after a cattle grid, the two routes separate. For the longer route continue reading from ★ below.

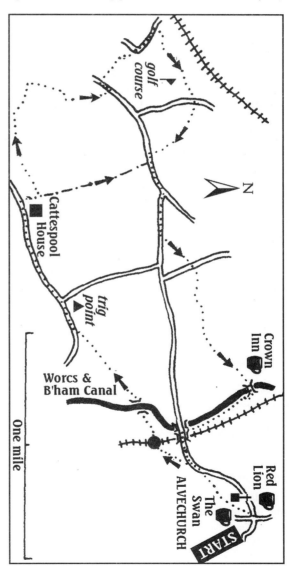

Following the **shorter route**, now turn right in front of a green barn. At the far corner of the barn, turn left and join a broad, farm lane soon to see the wooded Lickey Hills ahead on the horizon. After passing young hardwood plantations and nearing Wheeley Farm ahead, you may get distant views of the Cotswolds to the south-east, the Malverns to the south-west and the Abberley Hills to the west. On reaching a road, turn right, so rejoining the main route at ★ ★ on page 21.

★ For the **longer route**, turn left on reaching a green barn, go through a gate and continue along the bridleway, the surface of which may initially be muddy but improves as you continue along a green lane which is, essentially, the fenced-off margin of a meadow. After about 600 yards, pass through a gate and walk down a short, grassy slope beside young trees protruding from their growing tubes. After going through the next gate, turn to your right and follow the field margin until, between a cattle trough and a steep-roofed house, you proceed through a gate on your right. Continue ahead, walking round the perimeter of a field with a wire fence close at your left hand. When the second corner of the field is passed (and, if walking in early spring, you will have enjoyed the white flowers of a huge patch of blackthorn nearby), walk on for 35 yards where you cross a stile and plank bridge on your left.

In autumn, blackthorn (Prunus spinosa is the Latin name and this means 'spiny plum') provides us with sloes with which sloe gin may be made. It is also said to provide Irishmen with their shillelaghs.

Now continue with an intermittent hedge on your left until you reach a road which you join by means of a stile a few yards to your right. Having negotiated this stile, turn left and walk on for about 100 yards. Immediately beyond Blackwell Lodge, you climb a stile onto Blackwell Golf Course and continue straight ahead with a stream on your right. Having crossed several bright-green fairways (beware of flying golf balls!), turn right onto a lane and walk ahead on this for nearly 300 yards. When you come to the driveway of the Golf Club (which is directly opposite to the entrance to Blackwell Court, the International Scout Centre), turn right and proceed towards the clubhouse, this drive being a public right-of-way despite its lack of a sign to indicate this. Just before the clubhouse turn right through a metal, kissing gate and follow the clear, grassy path as it goes towards a pool and then swings to the left and gently curves its way across another part of this attractive golf course.

To your left is the railway line. The trains travelling towards Birmingham may be just recovering their speed after negotiating the famous Lickey Incline. The Bromsgrove to Blackwell section of the Gloucester to Birmingham railway was opened on September 17 1840. Just over two miles long and involving a 1 in 37.7 slope, it provided a severe test for the steam engines of those days. Ascending trains needed 'banking' (i.e. another engine would be added) and those descending would be subject to speed limits and special braking regulations. (For the enthusiast, Over the Lickey! by Smith and Harrison will be of interest.)

Having made your way over the final fairway, cross a stile by a holly bush, the lane adjacent to it and the stile which lies to the left of a large metal gate opposite you. Continue up a rough track to negotiate two more stiles, the second of which gives access to a large field. Here turn right and follow the margin of the field up the slope for a couple of hundred yards until you reach a stile. Climb over this and walk ahead to your next stile which is just to the right of the tall evergreen hedge which surrounds Wheeley Farm. On reaching a road, you turn left. When you reach the top of the slope and come to the entrance to Wheeley Farm, you are joined by those who have used the short-cut.

★ ★ Continue ahead and, at a road junction, veer right onto Scarfield Hill. Walk on for about 300 yards and continue until, soon after a house called 'The Stables', cross a stile on the left and take the short, enclosed path ahead which leads into a field. Now proceed with the hedge at your right hand, crossing five further stiles.

On the muddy approaches to one of these stiles, you will find planks laid to ease your progress. For this and other work done hereabouts, walkers are indebted to volunteers of the Alvechurch Village Society who have maintained waymarks, have replaced rickety stiles and who have undertaken drainage projects. Bravo!

After the final stile, cross a lane and take a gravel path which runs alongside a tall, brick wall past barn conversions. Another stile now leads to a meandering, grassy slope down which you go towards Alvechurch. The route of this path is fairly clear and, where there is doubt, waymarks are generally in evidence. About 100 yards after passing a tree-lined pool reach the far end of the field and here cross a stile by a gateway, veer half-left over the brow of a meadow and walk down to the near-end of a terrace of red-brick houses in Withybed Green. Walk on down the lane in front of the cottages and, shortly after the Crown Inn, cross a canal bridge and, on its far side, turn right onto the towpath and then left (i.e. away from the bridge) to walk along it.

On the opposite bank after 300 yards lies the remains of the old brickworks. Opened in 1860, it provided important employment here until about 1939. The canal was of vital importance to it, bringing in coal and taking away the bricks which had been made from clay extracted from the ground locally.

Follow the towpath to the next bridge (No. 60) where you leave the canal, walk up to the road, turn left and retrace your steps along Station Road, School Lane and Bear Hill into Alvechurch, those travelling by rail opting out at the station.

4

It's Not a Long Way to Tipperary!

Starting from Kenilworth Castle, a ramble that discovers some connections with a famous song.

Distance: 8¼ miles (6½ miles without diversion to Honiley church.)
Start: At the north side of Kenilworth Castle (described by Vivian Bird as 'Warwickshire's most romantic ruin'), opposite The Queen and Castle (GR279723).
Maps: Landranger 140; Pathfinder 955; Explorer 221.
Car Parking: For those visiting Kenilworth Castle, the Castle car park (on the south side of the Castle, off Castle Road) or the Gatehouse car park (on the north side) may be used. Otherwise, there is parking in Abbey Fields.
Public Transport: Bus service X16 (Coventry/Leamington/Stratford) – alight at Kenilworth Castle; Service 12 (Coventry/Leamington) – alight in Bridge Street, Kenilworth and walk through Abbey Fields to reach the castle (about a third of a mile).
Refreshments: The Queen and Castle (Beefeater), the Clarendon Arms and a teashop (by Kenilworth Castle); The Tipperary (Meer End).

WALKING away from the Queen and Castle, cross a shale car park and continue down a track which runs alongside the sandstone wall of the castle. On reaching the corner of the wall, turn right to walk in front of a pink, thatched cottage. On reaching a rough lane (Purlieu Lane), turn left and, after about 150 yards, cross a stile on your right. Now follow a path which slants half-left up the slope. Near the brow of the hill, you reach a gateway by a tumbledown barn. Pass through the gate and, confronted by two paths, select the one on your left. Walk ahead across two fields and, 40 yards after a stile by a sunken pool – the first of several such pools which you are soon to pass – turn right over another stile and go forward across two fields, aiming for a red-brick, multi-gabled building. On reaching a lane in front of these three houses, turn right for a few paces and then take the path on your left (signposted Meer End).

Walk on, with the field boundary on the left, and, just before reaching another sunken pool, you turn left to continue with the field boundary still at your left side. After the next pool, go a quarter-right across two fields to the far side of the second field where you turn left. Now walk on, by the hedge, for about 200 yards where, just beyond a larger pool, your path curves to the right to an old gatepost complete with hinge supports. Beyond this, turn right now to follow the field edge which soon curves left.

At the end of this field, about 200 yards before a red-brick farm, go through a gap and turn left to follow the meandering, lanky hedge. Go on to pass beneath electricity cables and, nearly 100 yards beyond another pool, reach a hedge elbow where you turn right to cross a field towards Rudfyn Manor. On reaching the far side, continue with the hedge at you left hand, soon passing in front of attractive barn conversions. Immediately beyond these, turn left and walk through a small spinney to reach a lane, onto which you turn left. Pass to the right of outbuildings and, at a white, five-barred gate turn right, keeping to the fence on your left.

The meadow on your left, and subsequent grassland, seem to accommodate large numbers of moles. Using their shovel-shaped forelimbs, they excavate underground tunnels in their quest for earthworms, insect larvae and slugs. Despite weighing only 3.5 oz, they can shift about 10 lbs of earth in 20 minutes. The spoil from their digging is pushed to the surface at intervals making the mole hills which are abundant here.

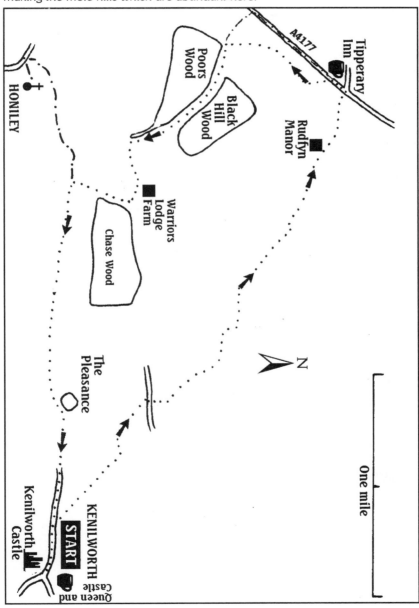

Just beyond the end of the mole meadow, go left and then right to continue on the same heading but now with the hedge on your right. Having crossed a stile beside a metal, farm gate, walk forward across the next field to find and climb over a pair of stiles to the left of some holly trees. Now walk straight ahead, hedge on your right, and, at the end of the second field, pass through a metal wicket-gate. Walk up a paddock and pass over a stile in its left-hand corner and another, five yards beyond it. Now aim for a stile beneath a pair of tall willow trees in the far right-hand corner of the next field, noticing an isolated wishing-well as you go. You now walk past Meer End Farm along an enclosed path and a lane to reach a road, the busy A4177.

Opposite you is the Tipperary Inn. On Walk 2 in More Country Walks, *you may have visited the grave of Henry ('Harry') Williams who, with his friend Jack Judge, wrote the World War I song 'It's a Long Way to Tipperary'. Harry lived at this pub (which, at the time, was called The Plough) with his parents, his father being the licensee. Sheila Bravington's excellent booklet, available in the pub, gives historical background to the story.*

From Meer End Farm, turn left (or, from The Tipperary, right) and, after 150 yards on the A4177 and just before reaching houses, you come to a gateway on your left which leads to an enclosed path. You have two options here.

- Option 1 should be taken if you are averse to stiles. However, the A4177 is a noisy racetrack and caution is recommended even if you remain on the grass verge. Ignoring the enclosed path, continue along the grass verge for nearly half-a-mile when, immediately past Croft Farm and opposite rugby pitches, you turn onto a bridleway on your left. Now continue reading from ★ on page 25.

- Option 2 is for those who are willing to climb numerous stiles (fourteen at the last count!) but enjoy relative quiet! Join the enclosed path mentioned

The Tipperary

above and, at the end of it, veer right to negotiate the first of the series of stiles. Follow the path which runs parallel to the road, crossing the numerous stiles and five driveways. Then, when you have passed through a field containing hundreds of newly-planted trees, bear left onto a gravel drive and soon curve to the right over a stream just beyond which you climb over a stile.

Walk on for 20 yards where you join an enclosed path. At the end of this, bear left onto another gravel drive and soon pass through a metal, kissing gate on the right. Cross a stile onto another enclosed path at the end of which you go ahead, with the hedge on your left. After the next stile, you turn left onto the bridleway used by those who have avoided the stiles.

★ Walk ahead on the bridleway which runs along the edge of Poors Wood. After about 250 yards, your path continues on a broad ride between the well-spaced trees of Poors Wood (on your right) and the more crowded inhabitants of Black Hill Wood (on your left). At a crossroads of forest tracks, ignore those to right and left and continue forward. After about 300 yards, you reach the end of the wood, with the ugly silos of Warriors Lodge Farm ahead of you across a field. Now bear right and walk round the margin of the field with a strip of woodland on your right.

At the end of the field, go through a hedge gap and turn left onto a farm track which leads to Warriors Lodge Farm. Pass to the right of the silos and

continue along a lane for about 100 yards to reach the corner of Chase Wood. Here turn right along a gravel driveway. Walk down this, noticing Honiley church coming into view half-right. Just over 200 yards beyond the bottom corner of the wood, you come to a bridleway which cuts across your track.

Here, the shorter and longer walks separate. For the shorter walk now continue reading from ★ ★ on page 26.

Following the **longer walk** (diversion to Honiley) turn right onto the bridleway. Near the end of the field, bear left to cross a footbridge and follow a hedge on your left which meanders up a slope, going well to the right of the church, there

Honiley Church

being no direct access from this side. When you reach a stile, climb over it and turn left. Two more stiles lead you to a lane onto which you turn left again. After 50 yards or so, turn left onto the first of two drives. This leads past the Lodges and the Malt House (the only buildings remaining from original Honiley House estate) to St John the Baptist's church.

The Latin inscription over the west door tells you that John Sanders built the church, at his own expense, in 1723. One of Sanders' friends was Sir Christopher Wren. It is said that whilst dining together, Wren drew the design of the church on the table cloth! But, according to L.F.Cave (Warwickshire Villages), 'legend is always more attractive than fact', the building probably being designed by Francis Smith of Warwick.

Nothing remains of St John's Well which is shown on the Pathfinder map so, having looked round the church, retrace your steps to where you left the shorter route. (In case you are unsure, walk down the drive to the lane, turn right and, in 50 yards, cross the stile on your right. At the end of the meadow, cross another stile and walk on until you reach another one on your right. Cross this and follow the hedge down the slope to the footbridge – ignoring a misleading waymark on an oak, partway down. (To your half-left, between Chase Wood and Warriors Lodge Farm, you may have a distant view of Coventry.) Having crossed the bridge, go ahead and, on reaching the hedge, go right and follow it to where the path from Chase Wood intersects.

Here the longer and shorter walks rejoin.

★ ★   Those who have been to Honiley now walk straight ahead. Those who have just come down the slope from Chase Wood turn left. You now begin a mile-and-a-half walk due east to Kenilworth, the Castle coming into view after the first stile which you encounter at about the halfway mark. The field beside which you walk for the first half-mile or so was created by felling the southern half of Chase Wood, the whole wood being shown on the 1991 Pathfinder. Continue on more-or-less the same heading and, after the third stile, aim ahead for another in the far corner of the field.

In this field, you walk between earthworks which mark the site of The Pleasance, a summerhouse built by Henry V as a retreat from the nearby – and much grander – Castle. The royal barge would have been used to ferry the royal party via the Great Pool, which surrounded the Castle, into the moat around The Pleasance. It was finally demolished by Henry VIII.

Having left The Pleasance field, continue on an enclosed path which takes you past High House Farm beyond which you rejoin Purlieu Lane, then turn right past the pink, thatched cottage along a path which leads you back to the Castle.

5

A Short Circuit from Beoley

This short walk would be ideal for a summer evening, but, even then, sensible footwear should be worn as there is some very uneven ground to cover.

Distance: 4 miles. Shorter route, starting at the Village Inn – ★ on page 30 – and omitting Beoley church, 2½ miles.
Start: Beoley church (GR065696).
Maps: Landranger 139; Explorer 220; Pathfinder 954 & 975.
Car Parking: Near Beoley church – but not during service times. (GR065696)
Public Transport: Midland Red 178 stops at Beoley Church.
Refreshments: The Village Inn, Beoley.

From the road running past Beoley church (B4101), walk through the car park towards the church of Saint Leonard.

This church was visited on Walk 9 of More Country Walks. *The graveyard at its west end is bedecked with snowdrops in springtime and it also contains a white tombstone commemorating P.C. James Davies who was murdered whilst on duty in 1885.*

Pass through the kissing gate in the car park's far right-hand corner. Bear right for about 25 yards and then walk down an avenue overhung mainly with hawthorn and, later, between tall poplars. At the end of the avenue, enter a field and follow the hedge as it curves off to the right. On reaching a dilapidated metal cattle trough beneath an oak, go forward over the top of a mound from where you may have good views half-right towards the Cotswolds. Do *not* attempt to cross the hedge on the other side of the mound but turn left and walk down beside the hedge to reach the bottom corner of the field. Here, 10 yards apart, you cross two stiles, the first being constructed of breeze-blocks. Now walk down a gentle slope across a large field aiming for a stile which lies some 50 yards to the right of the field's bottom left-hand corner. After crossing this, go down some (very-worn) steps, cross the deep-cut Beoley Brook via a footbridge and turn left immediately to cross another footbridge.

★ ★ It is here that those starting at the Village Inn and not wishing to visit the church continue their walk.

If your dog is with you, it will appreciate the lift-up devices at the ends of this bridge which will ease its progress. Many human walkers would welcome such assistance!

Now go half-right, aiming for a gap in the hedge which lies about 15 yards to the right of the far corner of this meadow. Having passed through this gap, turn left and walk beside the hedge to the field corner and climb over wooden palings. Now go half-right to negotiate a stile beside a metal gate. You now go through a series of three more paddocks, each time passing over a stile in their far-right corners. (Horses' hooves may have made your passage through these paddocks difficult – muddy in winter and uneven in summer – so take care!).

You finally emerge to cross a lane (Carpenters Hill) and go over a stile on the other side.

Now, hugging the tall boundary on your right, walk up a sloping field. Your next stile leads you into The Dingle, your path snaking its way up through woodland finally to reach Cherry Pit Lane between a pair of stately oaks, the right-hand one still bearing its old gate-hinges. Turn left and walk along Cherry Pit Lane for 400 yards.

Were it not for some distant road noise, you might find it hard to believe that you are not deep in remote countryside and that this lane, overhung with tall trees, is so near to one of the country's largest conurbations. The numerous pits in the area, from which this lane derives its name, were for used for the extraction of marl, a limey clay spread over the land to improve its fertility.

When you reach the driveway of Cherrypit (which is the next house after Cherrywood Cottage), leave the lane, turning right to join an enclosed path

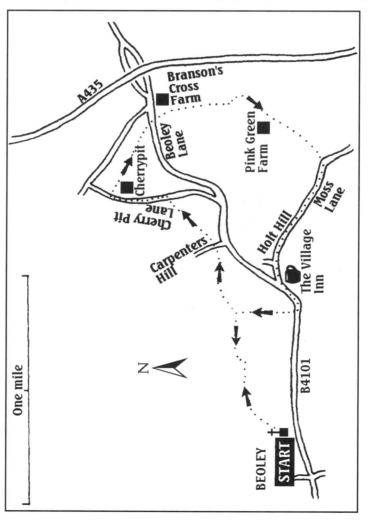

which lies to the left of the driveway. Continue on this path – there is an abrupt dog-leg when you are level with the house – and cross a stile at its end. Slightly left ahead of you, two fields away, is a red-brick farm (Branson's Cross Farm). Make a bee-line for this and, having crossed the two fields, cross a stile, the road (Beoley Lane – the B4101) and the stile at the other side. Now cross a pasture, aiming 30 yards to the right of a round, dark green crop store. After going across a farm track via two stiles, veer very slightly left to reach and negotiate another stile and then go straight ahead, your line being parallel to the hedge on your left and 20 yards from that hedge.

Having climbed over the stile at the end of this field, swing right and then left round a fenced-off duck pond. Your next stile lies 75 yards ahead of you. Beyond it, turn left and follow the hedge until you reach a lane (Pink Green Lane) onto which you turn right. Proceed for 150 yards along the lane where you pass through a white gate and continue walking beside tall, white-painted palings. After another 170 yards, just before the gate of Pink Green Farm, veer slightly left and right to continue on the same heading, now with wooden palings on both sides. At the end of these palings, go right and then (immediately) left to pass through a farm gate and walk ahead along a rough track with Redditch spread before you.

Just as the track begins to slope downwards, pause for a moment and study the horizon ahead. If visibility is good, you will see a water tower, the Malverns peeping up way behind it. Now trace the horizon along to your right and, just before it is interrupted by a patch of trees half-right, you will see the needle-shaped spire of Tardebigge church (visited on Walk 11 in Country Walks).

Continue down the track and leave it, as it swings sharply left, to go forward for a few paces to pass through a metal, wicket gate and turn right onto a lane (Moss Lane). Follow this narrow lane as it meanders between high banks. As it

Entrance to The Dingle from Cherry Pit Lane
From a sketch by Jimmy Yuill

widens and is flanked by houses, it becomes Holt Hill. Walk on, ignoring roads to right and left, until you reach the Village Inn.

★ *You may choose to start the walk here. If you leave your car here, please seek the landlord's permission first.*

Cross the road and turn left to walk along the pavement passing restored timber-framed properties. Soon after the road swings to the right, you reach a telephone kiosk beside a two-berth car park. Here turn right and continue on a path to cross two footbridges.

Though heavily overgrown in summer, this area abounds with the glossy yellow, star-like flowers of lesser celandine in springtime. One of its alternative names, 'pilewort', indicates the former use of its roots in alleviating a painful human condition.

After the second footbridge, pass through a kissing gate and continue on the same heading. The large meadow through which you now walk is, in summer, rich in wild flowers, but the path is fairly distinct, never straying more than ten yards or so from the left-hand hedge.

Beyond this hedge lies an old drovers' road, less easily passable than the path on which you are now walking, and now accommodating Beoley Brook. Apparently, in ancient times, long before the development of the Birmingham area, cattle were driven up this track for sale in Lichfield.

At the meadow's end, go over the footbridge on your left (i.e. the first one) and the stile just beyond it, so rejoining your outward route.

If you commenced at the Village Inn and do not wish to visit Beoley church, go over the footbridge ahead of you, i.e. the second one, and continue from ★ ★ *on page 30.*

Bear slightly left up to the top of the field where, having crossed two stiles, you turn left and walk beside the hedge up the incline. At the top, turn right and walk over the mound.

Ahead of you, a quarter-right, is Beoley Hall, now divided into flats. There has been a succession of buildings on the site dating back to the time of the Domesday Book. On the hillside beyond is the village of Rowney Green.

Bear left to pass the old cattle trough and then follow the hedge as it swings further left. You soon re-enter the avenue which leads you back to the church car park.

6

Down along Temeside

'Down along Temeside' is the title of a book written by Richard Holding who was a good friend of the author. It describes holidays during Richard's childhood beginning around the time of World War I and is a fascinating peep into rural social history. This walk savours the atmosphere of Richard's former haunts in this spectacular area of countryside near the extreme west of Worcestershire.

Distance: 7½ miles.
Start: Fox Inn near Hanley Child (GR670653).
Maps: Landranger 138; Pathfinder 973; Explorer 203.
Car Parking: Large lay-by opposite the Fox Inn on the B4204 near Hanley Child (GR670653).
Public Transport: Nothing suitable.
Refreshments: The Fox Inn.

FROM the Fox Inn forecourt turn left and walk westwards along the right-hand side of the road for about half a mile. Soon after the road begins to swing slightly right, take a <u>bridleway</u> on the right (NOT the footpath starting at the same point). Enter a field and walk down its right-hand margin, enjoying marvellous views over south Shropshire with the Clee Hills dominating the scene.

The nearer of the two hills is Titterstone Clee with Brown Clee, Shropshire's highest at 1772 feet, looking over its shoulder. These hills have a special fascination for the author who was born at Stoke St. Milborough, which shelters between them.

Follow the hedge and go with it as it swings left soon to enter an enclosed section of the bridleway through a wicket gate (which may be propped open). When the path emerges into the open, continue your descent into the Teme valley with the hedge now on your left. The hedge gradually curves to the right and, near the end of the field where the curve becomes more abrupt, go through a gap and turn right to walk down the slope. At the bottom of the field, turn left and continue along the meandering edge of a strip of woodland. When you reach the corner of the field, do <u>not</u> take the footpath ahead but turn left up the field again and, after 100 yards, turn right onto a farm track which skirts through Hillwood Farm beyond which it joins a lane.

This is pheasant country and you may have already noticed the variety of feeding devices which are meant to discourage these birds from defecting onto neighbouring property.

Continue down the lane and leave it, where it veers left, to go ahead through the middle one of three farm gates and follow the bridleway as it swings right. After passing through another gateway, turn left to walk along the top edge of an orchard at the end of which you pass through a gate and turn right. Follow the tractor track down and then to the left, soon passing a roofless cottage and continuing round the edge of the field. About 100 yards past the cottage and just beyond the top end of a very tall hedge, take the path which goes right, down into woodland, macabrely-named Death's Dingle. The path twists its way between the trees passing, just beyond a gate, a very deep gully on the left where ferns flourish. As you approach a second gurgling stream, you reach a path T-junction where you go left.

Soon after this, the path rises slightly to reach a road which you cross to go through the lower of the two gates, the one with the brick-built gateposts. Continue downwards, soon to join a smoothly-tarmacked road from which Abberley Tower (also known as Jones's Folly), passed on Walk 13 in *More Country Walks*, may come into view on the right. Continue past Eastham Grange with its pretty bell-tower and pass through the gate of Mill Cottage. Now go ahead, to the right of a wooden garage, pass through another gate and bear right to follow a track which leads around the edge of the field to reach a road. (The church tower half-a-mile ahead of you is at Lindridge, which is beyond the Teme.) Turn right along the road and, after a couple of hundred yards, you reach Lower House Farm, Eastham.

The converted barn by the roadside used to be an oast-house in which the hops which were grown locally were dried. Although still commonly grown on the farms over the river, the only hops in evidence on your walk are ones growing occasionally in the hedges. When the tower of the old oast-house fell down, its cowl was retained as a feature.

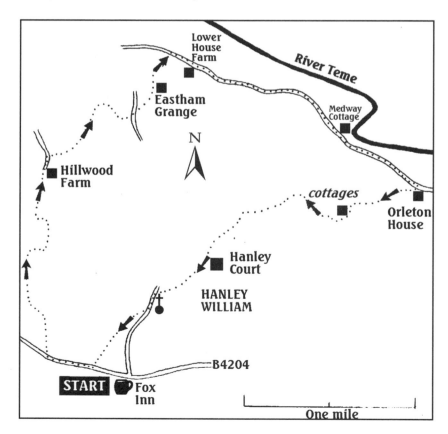

Continue along the lane for a further mile enjoying the quiet of the Teme valley with wooded slopes to your right and the village of Eardiston across the river to your left. When you reach the gate of Medway Cottage, the next-but-two house on your left, pause as it is mentioned in Richard Holdings's book.

One of Richard's childhood heroes was Tom Price. A man of all trades – joiner, metalworker, wheelwright, undertaker et al – Tom was also a regular poacher. However, when he was caught 'in the act', he and his wife were evicted from their home at Orleton Cottage and had to move into Medway Cottage which was close to the Holding family's holiday home, 'The Hut'.

To get your only sight of the Teme on this walk, take the footpath on the left immediately beyond Medway Cottage. After passing close to a bungalow on your right, go left and then immediately right over stiles, then to continue along the riverside to where the right-of-way ends where electricity cables cross overhead.

The banks of the river are, in summer, bedecked with Himalayan Balsam (its other name, Policeman's Helmet, aptly describing the shape of its flowers) and these largely obscure the river from view. It is here that Richard spent so many hours fishing in a river of which he wrote: 'We loved the Teme as it were our own'. It was also well-beloved of Edward Elgar who called it 'the most beautiful river that ever was'.

If you have followed the diversion to the river, when you get back to the road, turn left and continue, becoming aware of the extensive and fertile flood plain of the Teme on your left. As you go, you may see, ahead of you, the red-brick, battlemented tower of the chapel built in 1816, now converted for domestic use. When you reach the gates of Orleton House, overseen by lions rampant, turn right and walk up a roughly-tarmacked path.

100 yards after the path swings down to the left and about 20 yards before it starts to rise, go through a gap in the fence on the right. Walk straight forward aiming about 250 yards to the right of a pair of delightful cottages on the edge of woodland where you will find a stile in the top corner of the field, just beyond a leaking cattle trough. Cross this and turn right up the track and walk on for 100 yards. Here, go over a stile on your left (*easily missed*), bear right and walk on with the cottages' boundary just above you. At the top of the grassy slope, climb over the stile, now to follow a clear path which meanders upwards through mixed woodland.

'Their trees surround you, loom over you, press in from all sides. Woods choke off views and leave you muddled and without bearings. They make you feel small and confused and vulnerable, like a small child lost in a crowd of strange legs'. But this was Bill Bryson's opinion of woods recounted in his book called A Walk in the Woods in which he describes his hike along the 2,200 mile Appalachian Trail (he managed 40% of it) where the woods were a great deal larger than this one.

Please read the whole of the next paragraph before continuing.

When you reach a T-junction of paths in a small clearing go left briefly to reach a waymark post. *When last visited this post was loose making it susceptible to mischievous hands who may remove it or turn it round! Here take the right hand option and seek a thin path which slants off, steeply in places, up the incline. Soon you pass to the left of a multi-trunked holly tree and, in another 30 yards, you pass to the right of a coppiced oak with seven main trunks and then proceed for another 35 yards when you come to the edge of the woodland between a waymark post and a larch. This path is not particularly well defined. If at any point you are in doubt, note that essentially it follows a straight line up the slope to the edge of the woodland.*

Here, pause to regain your breath. A path runs straight up the field ahead of you. Follow it and, as you near the brow of the slope, a post beside a stile comes into view. However, when you reach the stile, do <u>not</u> cross it but turn left and follow the hedge now walking on level ground, the worst of your climb being now over. By way of a stile and plank bridge, go into the next field, still keeping the hedge near your right hand.

After a fine horse chestnut tree, the hedge swings right and then left but stay with it until, 50 yards after another cattle trough, you reach a farm track. Do not take the track which leads towards a house, but cross it and walk diagonally across the next field. As you go, you may notice, above the trees, the bell tower of Hanley Court to the left ahead of you and, over your left shoulder, you get a final glimpse of Abberley tower, flanked by Abberley Hill and Woodbury Hill, also explored on Walk 13 in *More Country Walks*. Ahead of you, a little elbow of woodland ending in a stout wooden gatepost, projects into the field. A few yards to the left of this gatepost you pass through a kissing gate, walk ahead with a pool to your right and emerge into a field.

Your next stile is three-quarters left just beyond tall evergreens. After the stile, bear right and pass in front of barn conversions, colourful in autumn with Virginia creeper. The top of the tower of Hanley William church is now in view in front of you. Cross two more stiles ahead and then aim across a large field for your next stile, which is just to the right of the grey barns of Church Farm. Walk on to reach a lane where you turn left, soon to enter the graveyard of All Saints' Church via a wicket gate.

This tiny church, with its chancel, the eastern part of its nave and its font bowl all dating from the twelfth century, is unpretentious yet charming. An interesting entry in one of its visitor's books was written by Dennis Shakeshaff of Sydney, Australia in September 1998. He was christened here in 1927 and he records that his grandfather, in about 1900, carved the pulpit from a single piece of oak. As you leave the churchyard, notice, parked on the north side, the church bier.

On reaching the lane again through the wicket gate, enjoy your near-final view of the Clee Hills and then turn left and walk on for about 150 yards where you go through the gate on the right-hand side of the road and then turn left. Walk beside the lane until, when you reach an oak tree with a pronounced leftward lean, you fork right to reach and cross a stile in the bottom corner of the field. Walk on for 40 yards where you must look out for an easily-missed footbridge and stile on your right. Cross these, turn left, cross another stile and walk up beside the hedge to reach a road. Here turn left and return to your starting place.

7

Some Ups and Downs from Piper's Hill

A walk that provides another opportunity to savour the view from Hanbury church.

Distance: 5½ miles.
Start: North car park of Piper's Hill Common (GR957652), which is also known locally as Dodderhill Common and Hanbury Woods.
Maps: Landranger 150; Pathfinder 974; Explorer 204.
Car Parking: At north (Stoke Prior) end of Piper's Hill Common on the B4091 Hanbury Road.
Public Transport: Bus service 140 (Droitwich/Bromsgrove) and 353 (Droitwich/Worcester). Start walking from ★ on page 37. The driver of the 140 bus should be able to drop you off at this point (the signed driveway to Valley Farm) which is about 300 yards north-west of the Jinney Ring Craft Centre on the B4091. The 353 bus stops at the Vernon Arms at the junction of the B4090 and the B4091. From here walk north-east along the B4091 for about three-quarters of a mile to reach the Jinney Ring Craft Centre. Pass this, continue along the B4091 and, about 100 yards after passing Hanbury Mount on the left, reach the entrance to Valley Farm.
Refreshments: The Gate Hangs Well and the Country Girl

Walk away from the road soon to join a rough lane which slants downwards and curves to the left leading to Knotts Farm. As you pass this, notice its farming memorabilia (including a pony-trap, a butter churn and several metal, milk churns) and an old petrol pump last used when a gallon of petrol cost 1/4½d! Continue ahead, walking on a track

Robert Goodchild with his 1936 Lagonda at Knotts Farm

some 20 yards inside the western edge of the woodland, noticing its ancient oaks and sweet chestnuts (with their spirally-grooved bark), some of which are thought to be over 300 years old.

In springtime, you may be fortunate enough to hear, but probably not to see, woodpeckers in this wood. Their rapid drumming on hollow trees is their way of announcing their territorial claims – estimated to be at 18 pecks per second! All three native woodpecker species, the green and the lesser and the greater spotted, have been seen here.

When you emerge from the woodland, go through a kissing gate and bear slightly right soon to join a path which leads you up to Hanbury Church which was visited on Walk 13 of *Country Walks*.

The Church of St Mary the Virgin stands majestically on a hilltop. Seats on the southern edge of its graveyard offer a useful site from which to enjoy, when visibility is good, outstanding views towards the Malverns, Bredon Hill and the Cotswolds.

From these seats, go through the adjacent metal, kissing gate and walk forward on flat ground for 40 yards. At this point, the land slopes abruptly downwards. Walk down the steep, grassy incline to reach a stile which lies some 25 yards to the left of the electricity post at the bottom of the slope. Cross this and descend stone steps to a road onto which you turn left.

Walk, with care, along this road for a quarter of a mile where you will see a footpath sign on your left, just beyond the driveway of The Old Church House. Join this footpath and follow it up a slope until you reach the Hanbury Road. Cautiously cross this.

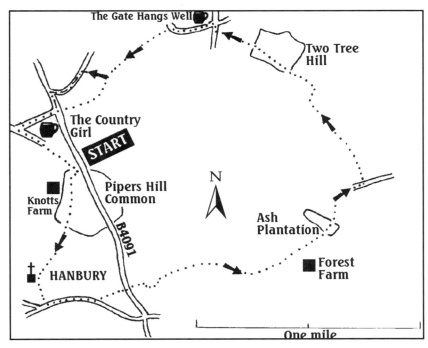

★ *Bus travellers start here.*

Join a private drive to Valley Farm which wanders down past several houses. At the end of the tarmac, cross a stile and continue beside a wire fence until you reach a stile and plank bridge. Cross this carefully and then veer slightly right, the direction of your path being indicated by a line of three widely-spaced trees, which formerly stood in a hedge. On reaching the far side of the field, climb over a stile, walk across a bridleway and then negotiate two more stiles opposite.

With your back to the last stile, go a two-thirds left up the slope (marked Forest Hill on the map but now almost devoid of live trees), near the brow of which you will reach a stile. Ignoring the waymark on the right, cross this stile and go ahead on the left-hand one of a pair of footpaths. At the end of this, go through a farm gate, cross a wide (and sometimes muddy) tractor track (which leads to Forest Farm) and pass through another gate at the other side.

Now walk ahead with the field boundary at your right hand until you enter Ash Plantation via a stile. Paths in this wedge-shaped spinney are somewhat indistinct but you bear very slightly left for your next target which is a footbridge and stile some 50 yards from the wood's far right corner. Having climbed over this, go straight across the next field to another stile which leads you into Foster's Green Meadows Nature Reserve. (If crops prevent you from using the direct route to this Reserve, you may be forced to go right from the stile out of Ash Plantation and walk round the field's periphery.) In the Reserve, go right for 10 yards and then left to reach, in about 100 yards, the main gate.

This Nature Reserve is managed by the Worcestershire Wildlife Trust and is considered to be one of the finest examples of lowland grassland in the U.K. Its rare plants include meadow saffron (or autumn crocus) which can be found here in greater abundance than anywhere else in Britain. This plant, which is poisonous to stock, produces its flowers long after its leaves have died off.

Beyond the gate, walk forward, soon to reach a lane. Continue down this for about 100 yards where you go left through a gate. Now aim for a double stile ahead and, after that, walk to a gateway across the next field. Having passed through this, continue with the hedge on your right until, near the end of the second field, you reach a gate by a footpath signpost. Go through the gate and go half-left to pass through a metal gate. (Take care to chose the correct path – there are several waymarks here!) Now walk ahead for just over 200 yards, with the hedge near your right hand, to reach and climb over a stile on your right near the end of the field.

You are now on Two Tree Hill – another misnomer for, in contrast to Forest Hill where trees were sparse, you are now in a flourishing hardwood plantation.

Inside the wood, of the several paths leading from the stile, choose the one on the extreme left. This will lead you over the brow of the hill to a stile from which, on clear days, you may have good views westwards of Abberley and Woodbury Hills and, further to the right, Shropshire's distant Wrekin. Cross the stile and, walking in the direction of a large, white factory building about a mile ahead, descend through two fields to reach a road via a kissing gate. Here turn right, in 100 yards or so reaching a pub on the cross roads.

The Gate Hangs Well has a long history. Unfortunately, a relative of the proprietor was not able to explain the name but he was adamant that the building is haunted!

At the crossroads, turn left and continue for about 300 yards until, 50 yards beyond Brookhouse Farm, you cross a stile on your left. Now aim for a stile in this field's far right-hand corner after which you continue up the gradual incline with the hedge at your right hand. After the next gate, you have two options.

Option 1: In the summer, when mud is but a distant memory, go slightly left to cross a complex stile after which you walk half-left towards two farm gates. Go through the one on the left to walk along a broad cattle track at the end of which two more gates lead you into a field down which you walk. On reaching the Hanbury Road, cross it to enter Sharpway Gate alongside the Country Girl pub.

Option 2: The cattle track mentioned above can be, for some of the winter months, an impassable morass and is to be avoided. So, continue slightly right up the slope to climb over waymarked paddock railings close to an electricity supply post. Go half-right and, by way of two stiles (the second of which has a very user-friendly top rail), join a road. Turn left into this and, at the next T-junction, turn left, cross the Hanbury Road and soon turn right into Sharpway Gate beside which is the Country Girl pub.

Walk down Sharpway Gate and follow it as it swings left at the next junction. After the last house (Farthings Green), you meet two paths going into the wood. Take the one on the right (waymarked) and follow it as it snakes its way through the wood. When you reach a rough, vehicle track, turn left to return to your starting place. (Those who have travelled by bus should, when they reach the track, join it and go ahead towards Knotts Farm, then continue reading from the start of the chapter.)

8

Preston Bagot and Lowsonford

A pleasant walk through Warwickshire villages.

> **Distance:** 4½ miles or 5½ miles.
> **Start:** Preston Bagot , near bridge 47 on the towpath of the
> Stratford-upon-Avon canal alongside Preston Bagot Bottom Lock (No.
> 38) (GR175655).
> **Maps:** Landranger 151; Pathfinder 975; Explorer 220.
> **Car Parking:** Roadsides beyond Manor House, Preston Bagot in
> cul-de-sac off A4189 Henley-in-Arden to Warwick road 1½ miles from
> Henley. (GR175655)
> **Public Transport:** Adds 2½ miles. Rail or bus service X20
> (Birmingham/Stratford) to Henley in Arden. To reach the main walk see
> the box on page 43.
> **Refreshments:** The Fleur-de-Lys, Lowsonford.

WALK away from the bridge with the Stratford-upon-Avon Canal on your left and, on reaching the next bridge (No. 46), cross to the other side of the canal.

Immediately take a path down from the towpath soon to reach and cross a footbridge over a stream. After climbing over the next stile, go straight ahead across the field where you turn right and walk up the slope with its rather overgrown hedge at your left hand. This hedge was mentioned on Walk 12 in *Country Walks* because of the rich bounty of autumn fruits that it provides for the local bird life. At the top of the field, bear left through a gap and then follow the well-trodden path ahead to reach a lane onto which you turn right.

★ *Public transport users join and end the walk here.*

Immediately on your left is a short drive which leads to All Saints' Church, Preston Bagot, topped by a shingled bell turret. It was built by the Normans on this hilltop and affords good views to the south.

Continue along the twisting lane until, after nearly 350 yards, you take the left fork and pass a no-through-road sign. When the tarmac ends, continue on a rough track (Preston Field Lane), crossing a stream by a footbridge *en route* and finally reaching a road. Here turn left and walk on for nearly a quarter of a mile. Just before the road swings to the left, turn into a farm lane on your right leading to Coppice Corner Farm, here joining the Heart of England Way.

About 80 yards beyond a bridge over a disused railway, turn right through a metal wicket gate and follow a track which, at the far end of the field, swings left. Beyond metal gates turn right and follow the hedge for 40 yards where you pass through a gap and begin a slow ascent on the edge of a wood. After a further 30 yards, go left into the wood and then right to continue on a clear path straight ahead to the top of a long incline. Here, cross a stile and continue, now with the wood's edge on your right. On reaching a stile complex, turn right and, after about 75 yards turn left and walk down to the left of an electricity pole, cross a stile and make for another which is just to the left of a red-brick house.

Join the lane and walk down towards the village of Lowsonford and, at a crossroads, turn right soon to pass or make use of the Fleur de Lys pub.

At one end of this old coaching inn, where a former smithy stood, you are proudly told that Roland Fletcher Brookes, a former landlord, began the production of Fleur de Lys meat pies here and you are given some production statistics. The floor levels changing abruptly in several places, there are plenty of steps for the unwary and also low beams, customers being warned on one of them to 'Duck or grouse'!.

About 100 yards beyond the Fleur de Lys, fork left and cross a canal bridge. Here the two routes diverge.

The Fleur de Lys

'Meat Pies' Display in the Fleur de Lys

For those using the **shorter route,** take the gate on the right to join the towpath and make your way back down the canal to your starting point.

If you intend to walk the slightly **longer route**, continue along the road until, just before the church of St Luke, take a stile on your right.

The uncomplicated church of St Luke was re-opened in April 1999 after some years of closure. Its simple font is a staddle stone with its top plate turned upside down.

Having crossed the stile, walk up the slope aiming for the nearest electricity post passing, on your left, a hollow which the local platoon of the Home Guard (or Local Defence Volunteers, as they were originally named) used as its rifle range during World War II. At the top, walk on with the wire fence on your left, soon to cross a double stile in the boundary ahead. Now bear right towards the hedge and walk with it until, about 150 yards beyond the next stile, you strike off, half left, down the slope. At the bottom, go through a hedge gap and proceed with the hedge on your right.

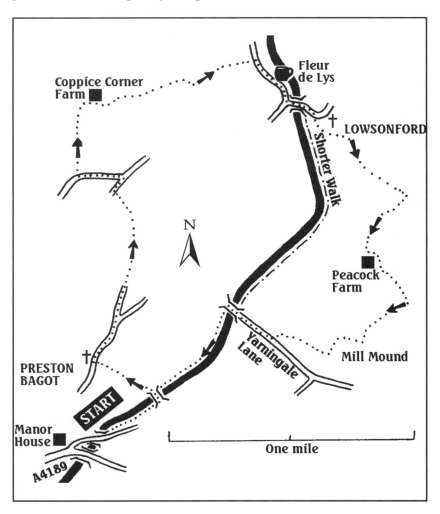

When you reach the corner of the field, bear right along a narrow strip of grassland. At the end of this, ignore the two footpaths on your left and go straight ahead through a metal wicket gate which is ornamented with horseshoes. Continue on a bridleway which, like most rights-of-way of its type, can be muddy in winter. At the end of this enclosed track, veer left past a farm (Peacock Farm). Immediately beyond the farm, pass through a gate on your right and walk down the field to cross a stile and plank bridge in its bottom right-hand corner. Now go three-quarters left up the incline, pass through a gap in paddock railings and then continue ahead for nearly 100 yards to cross a stile to the right of the garden of a timber-clad house.

Turn right and walk down the next field at the bottom corner of which you cross a couple of stiles and a footbridge. Now proceed with the hedge on your left for about 75 yards where you pass through a gate and continue ahead, soon with a wire fence at your right-hand side. When you reach a stile, cross it, turn right and walk in front of a farmhouse and another house (Oaktree Farm) and continue on a rough path for another 70 yards. Here, you veer left between wooden palings to enter woodland and join a twisting, uphill path. (Be alert for there is a network of paths on this slope!)

A dozen yards after the palings, your path swings up to the left and, in another 30 yards, goes off to the right soon passing more palings. Follow the path as it again swings uphill and go ahead over a cross path near the top. Very soon you emerge from the wood and bear right onto Mill Mound, a grassy, open space which is equipped with seats where you may wish to pause. Walk across to a seat on a concrete base which is to the left of the mound.

Although no excavations have been made, it is thought that Mill Mound may have been used as a look-out post by the Romans. The seat commands particularly good views to the south-west and, on clear days, you may see Bredon Hill and the Malverns. A plaque makes another reference to the Home Guard for it records that one of its observation posts stood on this spot during World War II. Despite its name, there is no evidence of Mill Mound ever being equipped with a windmill.

About 50 yards behind the seat (and on the opposite side of the mound) pass through more palings and follow a path which twists its way down to the north-west side of Yarningale Common, emerging near a house called Ben Side. Turn left along a gravel track to reach a lane. (In case you came down from the Mill Mound on another route and need to get back on track, this is called Yarningale Lane.) Here, turn right and walk down the lane until, in about a quarter of a mile, it ends at some cottages. Join a path which veers to the right of the cottages. This soon leads up steps to a little cast-iron aqueduct carrying the canal over a stream. Here turn left, cross the bridge and again turn left, now in front of Bucket Lock Cottage. The shorter route has now joined you as you walk along the towpath to reach your starting point near lock 38.

If you are using public transport, when you reach bridge 46 turn right off the towpath and then continue reading from the second paragraph on page 39.

Car users follow the towpath down to where you started your circuit.

For public transport users

From Henley-in-Arden station go down the station approach to join Station Road and after a few yards turn right along Swan Croft. Follow the Heart of England Way waymarks to reach the High Street.

Cross the road and turn right, then left along Beaudesert Lane passing St John's Church. Pass Alne Close and continue forward along the enclosed path, signed as a cycleway. Cross the end of a road, walk around two sides of school grounds to reach and cross a road and go into playing fields. Bear left and then ascend steps to enter a field. Go forward to cross a stile and now walk with a hedge on the left. On reaching a lane go right for a few yards, then left into a field. Now walk with a hedge on the left through three fields. Leave the third field by a stile, go forward a few yards, then right along an enclosed path, leaving it by a stile on the left.

Go straight forward across a field to cross a stile. Now walk with a hedge on the left through four fields. In the fourth field walk slightly right aiming towards the right of a farm ahead. Cross a stile and walk with a hedge on the left, cross a short field, pass a cottage and reach a lane. Cross this and ascend an enclosed path to reach Preston Bagot church. Enter the churchyard by a kissing gate, walk along the right side of the churchyard, go through a parking area to reach a lane and turn left along this. Now pick up the walk from ★ on page 39.

Returning to Henley go through Preston Bagot churchyard, leaving it through a kissing gate and walking briefly with a fence on the right, then forward to leave the field by a kissing gate. Descend the enclosed path, cross a lane into a field, pass the cottage on the right and cross a stile, then forward and across another stile. Now walk with a hedge on the right through a field, then go straight across the next field. Cross a stile, pass a stile on the right and now walk with a hedge on the right through four fields. In the next field go straight forward, cross a stile and turn right. Cross another stile on the left and walk with a hedge on the right through three fields. Reach a road, go right for a few yards, then turn left and walk with a hedge on the right. Almost at the end of the field cross a stile on the right, go forward across another stile and descend steps. Cross the playing field, cross a road and join the path to walk around the school and back to Beaudesert Lane and Henley High Street. Turn right, then just past the White Swan turn left, signed Shallowford Court, following this back to Station Road and the railway station.

9

A Claverdon Circuit

An undulating walk, mainly on field paths, exploring quiet Warwickshire villages, the longer option being particularly attractive at bluebell-time.

> **Distance:** 7½ miles. Shorter route 4½ miles.
> **Start:** Church of St Michael and All Angels, Claverdon (GR198645).
> **Maps:** Landranger 151; Pathfinder 975/976; Explorer 220/221.
> **Car Parking:** Roadsides near Claverdon church.
> **Public Transport:** Rail: (Adds about one mile.) From Claverdon station, walk up Station Road on the pavement for about 500 yards when, just before a white house called Hunters Lodge, turn left onto a footpath. Reaching a field turn right and walk with a hedge on your right up through three fields to Park Farm where you join the walk at ★.
> **Refreshments:** The Red Lion in Claverdon.

In the chancel of Claverdon church are important memorials. An elaborate one is that of Thomas Spencer, who died in 1586 and was an ancestor of Diana, Princess of Wales. Another commemorates Sir Francis Galton FRS, cousin of Charles Darwin, who died in 1911. His memorial tablet recounts that 'many branches of science owe much to his labours' but he may be best remembered for his pioneering work on fingerprinting.

Leaving the churchyard through its main gate, turn left and walk along the road for nearly 100 yards where you turn right into the driveway of Park Farm. After about 60 yards, cross a stile to the right of a farm gate.

★ Rail travellers start here.

Now walk diagonally down the field on your right to its far corner.

At the time of writing, this field was being re-seeded after the removal of its previous crop which was lawn turf, not an unusual product in these parts, as you may see later.

After passing through a wicket gate, walk right and then left to pass between a pool and a hedge. Now continue down through two fields with the hedge at your right hand. Cross the railway line with care and continue, on the same bearing, beside a drainage ditch. On reaching a stream, go to the left and, in about 75 yards, cross a footbridge.

On one of his excursions along this route, a mink was seen near this stream by the writer. This species was introduced from America to the UK to be bred for its fur. Some of the animals have escaped and others have been released by activists. The result is that the mink is a pest which, having no natural predators, is having a serious impact on the environment, killing fish and a wide variety of birds and small mammals.

Beyond the footbridge, go *slightly* right up the next field and, having crossed a stile, negotiate a steeper gradient soon to walk to the right of a spinney and continue on a broad, tractor track with the hedge on your left. Cross a road and the stile opposite and then bear a little to the right across the next field. (*Should this footpath be obstructed – a recent crop was the walker-unfriendly oilseed rape! – turn right along the road and, after a little over 250 yards, turn left onto a track signed Manor Farm which leads to the church.*) If you have not been obliged to divert, after the next stile aim just to the left of a bungalow soon to bear left onto a driveway which leads past a farm pool. On reaching a road, turn right and after about 45 yards, turn right again and walk up a slope towards the wooden bell-turret of Wolverton church.

In the ancient wooden porch of the church, note the advice given by the text: 'That thou injure no man, dove-like be, and serpent-like that none may injure thee'. Inside, you will find a well-maintained, barrel-roofed church of charming character.

From the church, continue up the tarmac path, pass through a metal kissing-gate and bear half-right across a paddock to pass through a wicket gate. Now walk up a slope, a straggly hedge on your right. You will pass *en route* the Wolverton Millennium Seat – an interesting practical work of art. At the end of the field, where the Malverns may come into view 30 miles away, a quarter-left, cross a stile and turn right. Walk on with the field boundary on your right. After climbing over a stile, go down half-left across the slope to reach a road. Cross this and, a little to your left, go between trees to reach and cross another stile.

Now go half-left across a meadow, aiming for the right-hand end of a hedgerow where you pass through a gate. Walk on, boundary on left, to reach and cross the railway track. Go ahead for a few yards to cross a footbridge and then continue beside a hedge and stream for about 35 yards. When the hedge angles off to the right, walk straight up the slope (on the line of a

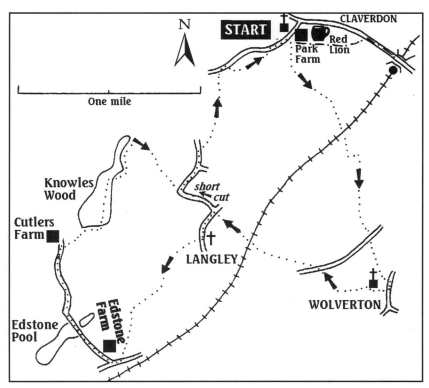

The Millennium Seat at Wolverton

recently-removed hedgerow) aiming for an old, corrugated-iron shed. Cross a stile by the shed and walk ahead to reach a lane. It is here that the two options separate.

If you wish to follow the **shorter route** *turn right here and, in a few paces turn left to walk up another lane. When, after about a quarter of a mile, this angles sharply to the right, re-join the instructions at* ★ ★ *on page 48.*

For the **longer route**, turn *left* and walk for about 300 yards through the pretty village of Langley. Soon after walking beside its sunken stream, you reach on the left the tiny, brick-built church of St Mary which seats no more than thirty worshippers and is immaculately maintained. Here turn right up a bridleway to the right of the white-painted Bridle Cottage. After about 350 yards, just before the bridleway narrows and becomes overgrown, cross a stile on your left and then slant off half-right to walk down a slope and then, between a huge bramble/blackthorn thicket and a thin stream, continue to a stile.

As you walk towards the stile, you may be walking between daisies which flower throughout the year. Because they are looked upon as weeds on our lawns, their beauty is often overlooked. The name is thought to have originated from the fact that they close their flowers at night and open them in the day – hence 'daisy' which may be a corruption of "day's eye".

Having gone over the stile, turn right, walk along the field edge and soon pass through a hedge gap at the end of the field. Immediately opposite is a stile with a railway-sleeper step. Cross this and proceed slightly right across a reedy meadow to reach and cross a footbridge. Continue on the same line as the bridge to walk past a row of five oak trees which must once have marked a field boundary. (The woodland to your half-left on the horizon is Austy Wood, visited on Walk 15 in *Country Walks* and on Walk 12 in this book.) Near the fifth tree cross a stile and beyond it, keep on the same bearing, aiming for an old oak. When you reach this, bear slightly right to walk past old tree boles, soon to reach a road. Turn right onto this and walk on for nearly 150 yards, passing

Edstone Farm *en route*. Turn right onto a tarmacked lane to Cutlers Farm. After a quarter of a mile, by means of two stone bridges you cross the reed-fringed Edstone Pool with its variety of waterfowl.

The moorhen can easily be distinguished from its close relative the coot, the former having a red forehead and the latter a white one. However, behaviourally they are very different. The dapper moorhen flicks its black and white tail as it swims quietly about its business. The coot is a little larger and is the 'bovver boy' of the pool, in spring constantly squabbling and chasing its fellows.

Edstone Pool in springtime

Beyond the pool, the lane swings right and you stay on it for about half a mile as it twists its way up through sheep pastures towards Cutlers Farm passing, on the way, an ancient oak which must have been on duty there for many, many years. About 100 yards before you reach the cream-painted farm, leave the tarmacked surface and follow the bridleway as it goes right. Walk up the slope, keeping the hedge on your left and, on reaching the bluebell-rich Knowles Wood, bear right to walk along its southern edge. After about 200 yards and shortly before a metal gate, leave the bridleway and cross a stile on your left. Your path now meanders gently upwards just inside the wood's eastern margin between, in their season, a rich floral display of lesser celandines, primroses, wood anemones, greater stitchwort and bluebells (with their occasional white variants).

On the path, look out for the two-slotted footprints of deer. The author had brief glimpses of deer on his last two visits, the most recent being of a muntjac which is as big as a medium-sized dog.

About 20 yards before the north boundary of the wood, follow the advice of a waymark post and turn right where you soon walk beneath a huge holly tree. When you emerge from the wood, continue ahead between hawthorn scrub (on your right) and bramble thickets (on your left). After 100 yards or so, follow the well-worn path as it goes left and loosely follows the woodland edge. After about 450 yards, you come to a path T-junction. Here you go right and, about 250 yards after passing an area of young oaks, climb over a stile by a farm gate. Your enclosed path now gradually slopes down and, soon after another stile, you join a road and turn left.

· ★ ★   *The shorter route rejoins here.*

Pass Hunters Lodge (the second house of that name that the rail travellers will have seen) and walk up the lane noticing its interesting houses. On arriving at a T-junction, turn left (signposted 'Claverdon 1½') and walk up a sharp incline for about 150 yards. Near the top of the bank, immediately after The White House, join a track on the right. After the second stile, swing right for 30 yards to cross another one. Beyond this, you go down a slope with the hedge on your left and with the tower of Claverdon church now in view.

Cross a footbridge and then begin a climb up the other side, keeping the field edge near your right hand, with the flowers of gorse ablaze in places as you go. After a little over 500 yards, you reach a road onto which you turn right. After 75 yards, immediately beyond the driveway of a house named Rookley, go through a green, farm gate on your right. After 100 yards, cross a stile on your left and walk across a field, aiming for its far left corner. Here cross a stile and walk the few strides needed to get back to the church.

For refreshment continue past the church and turn right at the T-junction. The Red Lion is a little way down the hill.

You are now back in Claverdon at the start of your walk. Claverdon was, as Clavendone, mentioned in the Domesday Book, the name possibly being derived from the words Clover Down.

If you have travelled by train walk on past the church and, in 100 yards, turn right towards Park Farm. After 60 yards, go over a stile to the left of a farm gate and retrace your steps to Station Road and your transport.

10

A Two-County Walk

This walk, which explores villages between Astwood Bank and Coughton Court, astride the Warwickshire – Worcestershire boundary, is mainly on quiet field paths.

Distance: 8 miles.
Start: By the telephone kiosk opposite the White Lion in Astwood Bank (GR044624).
Maps: Landranger 150; Pathfinder 975; Explorer 220.
Car Parking: Free car park in Astwood Bank at the intersection of the A441 Evesham Road and the B4092 Sambourne Lane.
Public Transport: Midland Red West service 70 (Redditch-Astwood Bank). Alight in Avenue Road, Astwood Bank, and walk forward to the junction with Evesham Road (The Bell Inn on the corner), cross Evesham Road, turn left for about 25 yards, then turn right to cross a stile and walk down an enclosed path. Now continue from ★ below.
Refreshments: The White Lion and the Bell Inn in Astwood Bank, the Green Dragon in Sambourne and the Throckmorton Arms in Coughton.

FROM the telephone kiosk walk southwards (towards Evesham) and, 130 yards past the War Memorial, cross a stile on your left and walk down an enclosed path.

★ After crossing another stile (and the county boundary), continue straight ahead and, at the end of the field, cross a lane and walk on, now with the hedge on your right. Having walked more-or-less in a straight line from the A441 for about half a mile, you reach the end of the next field where you go through a wide gap and then branch half-right to reach and pass through a kissing gate. Proceed with an evergreen hedge at your left hand and, 20 yards after it goes left, turn right through another kissing gate.

Walk on, with the hedge on your left, until, at the end of the third field, you cross a stile and continue forward, aiming for the (black-and-white) Green Dragon. Just beyond the red-brick Sambourne church, you reach a road intersection. Bear slightly left and walk across the village green in the direction of a bus shelter, on your way noticing the plaques beside the trees and the board about the history of the village green.

On your left stands a fine black-and-white house (Yew Tree Cottage) with a thatched roof. Incorporated into the thatch are two

Yew Tree Cottage

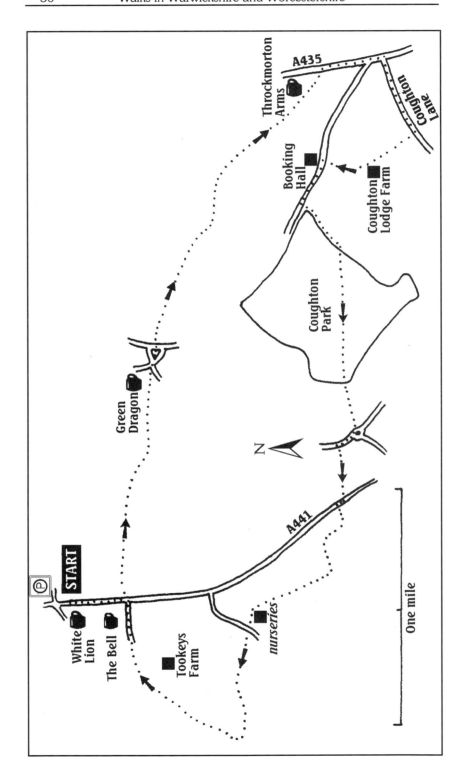

straw pheasants which, when the roof was recently replaced by Max Grindlay, a thatcher from Long Itchington, took the place of four ducks which were the previous thatcher's 'signature'.

Take the tarmac track to the left of the bus shelter at the end of which a stile leads you into a narrow field. Just before a stile at the end of this field, you are crossing a dismantled railway track, evidence of which is the bridge to be seen on your right. Negotiate this stile and the one straight ahead in the next field. After crossing a lane, continue with a stream on your left. Near the end of the farm buildings of Sambourne Hall, veer right and left to resume your former heading on a wide tractor track.

You soon pass a red barn in front of which you will notice an old cast-iron water pump, plastic replicas of which are commonly to be seen in garden centres on their way to give suburban gardens an 'olde-worlde' look

Stay on the tractor track until, at the bottom of a slope, you cross a stream and another stile beside a gate. Now bear half-left to continue your walk with a hedge at your right hand. At the end of this field, turn left for 35 yards to climb over a stile. Keeping the boundary fence on your right, continue until, just after the end of this long field go through a gate, continue forward for about 35 yards and carefully cross a stream by way of a plank bridge which can be very slippery after wet weather.

Proceed onwards, soon noticing, in the boundary near you right hand, a dilapidated, wooden five-barred gate (see note on page 77). At the end of this field, you will see another such gate, still functioning, but clearly at the end of its working life. Climb over the stile to its left and continue beside a stream, ignoring a wooden footbridge (unless you wish to take refreshment at the Throckmorton Arms). When you reach the busy A435, cross it with care, turn right and walk on with, across parkland to your left, Coughton Court. It was here that the wives of the Gunpowder Plotters stayed while their husbands went about their business at Westminster in November 1605.

The spotted sheep, which you may see in the parkland, are Jacob Sheep. They are said to have originated in Old Testament times. Chapter 30 of the Book of Genesis records how, as a reward for his good work, Laban took 'every speckled and spotted sheep' from his flock and gave them to his nephew Jacob to set up his own flock. Thus isolated, the breed became established.

If you choose to visit this National Trust property, you may do so via the metal, kissing gate which you reach after about 200 yards. Otherwise, continue beyond the gate for a further 150 yards where you will see a fenced-off monument.

This consists of the steps and base of the shaft of a medieval cross which marks the spot where travellers prayed for safe passage as they went through the Forest of Arden.

Now go back a few yards to the pedestrian crossing and cross the A435 again, then turn left to reach and turn right along Coughton Lane. Leaving the rumbling traffic behind, opposite the school on your left you will see two houses with thatched roofs, the second 'signed' with a straw pheasant, the garden displaying an authentic-looking water pump. Continuing up the gradual slope, you may notice, just before you cross the disused railway again, a house on the right with an unusual name. The garage of house 38 carries a number plaque from the old London and North Western Railway (which disappeared as a separate company in 1923).

Walk ahead for about 200 yards at which point you turn right onto a rough tractor track (NOT the driveway of the adjacent house). When the track veers left towards Coughton Lodge Farm, go straight ahead across the field, passing between the farm buildings and an isolated oak. Bear right onto a concrete roadway soon to pass across a well-defined moat.

One suggestion is that the moat encircled the original farmhouse which disappeared long ago. Another is that it was used, in the dim and distant past, to corral cattle at night to prevent them straying off into the Forest of Arden.

Continue beyond the moat and, on reaching a road (Sambourne Lane), turn left.

On your right, you have your final encounter with the dismantled railway. Beyond the white-painted 'Station House' (in which the stationmaster lived) is 'Booking Hall'. At the entrance gate there is a most interesting plaque from the Somerset and Dorset Railway. This tastefully-modernised railway building is now owned and occupied by Mr Thomas Hunt. Mr Hunt remembers, as a boy, travelling on this railway which connected Birmingham, via Redditch, to Ashchurch, near Tewkesbury. A victim of Dr Beeching's axe, the last train passed here in 1964.

After walking up Sambourne Lane for just over 300 yards, turn left onto a deeply-rutted bridleway which runs along the margin of woodland called Coughton Park. In a further 400 yards, turn right as the bridleway swings into the forest and follow it for over half a mile in a straight line, ignoring forestry tracks going off left and right. After a final downhill section which can be very muddy in winter, you emerge from the woodland and walk straight ahead, keeping to the left of the field boundary which is marked by a row of oaks.

When the boundary goes off to the right, continue ahead on your original bearing to cross the field to a road junction. Here, walk along the road on your right for about 150 yards (where the road bends right) and turn left to walk up a sloping field with the hedge on your right. At the top of the slope, you cross the boundary between Warwickshire and Worcestershire again and bear right to walk through scrubland to the A441 which runs along the Ridgeway. Cross the road with care to reach the pavement, turn right and, after walking for 60 yards, turn left onto a private road immediately before Marlborough House.

Having left the A441, after about 100 yards bear slightly right and then left. To the right of metal farm gates and a stile (which you ignore), pass through a kissing gate. Walk along an enclosed path, passing through another kissing gate. Immediately beyond the next stile, turn left and continue with the hedge on your left, trying to ignore the unsightly pylons which march off diagonally to the right. At the corner of the field, walk between the legs of one of the metal monsters and turn right to join the Monarch's Way, a long distance path from Worcester to Shoreham that follows the route taken by Charles II after his defeat at the Battle of Worcester. You pass through a kissing gate beyond which a seat overlooking a pool may afford welcome rest.

Continue with the hedge on your left, pass through another kissing gate and resume your former heading, now with the hedge on your right. Continue over a succession of four stiles and, after passing some very large glasshouses, turn left to walk between more glasshouses and through the premises of Botany Bay Nurseries to reach a road. Cross the road, climb a stile and enter the busy builders' yard of S.E.Davis and Son. Ltd. Stay close to the left-hand boundary, passing close to a large collection of vintage earthmoving machinery, caterpillar tractors and steam engines belonging to Mr R.H.Davis. At the far end of the yard – it is about 200 yards long – a stile (✕) leads into a field.

(It is possible that the path will, sometime in the future, be diverted around the builders' yard to rejoin the route at the stile marked ✕ above. Look out for waymarks!)

After crossing the stile, follow the boundary down to the bottom left-hand corner of the field and, after negotiating another stile, aim for the next field's bottom left-hand corner. Here turn right to reach and go through a gate. Ford a small stream (which might perhaps disappear in a prolonged dry period) and turn right. Follow the stream and, after the next stile (beside a gate), go left and follow the hedge until you come to a stile to the left of a large oak. Cross this and bear half-right up the slope ahead of you, making for the stile halfway along the fence at the top.

As you climb the slope, the splendid black-and-white building to your right is Tookeys Farm. At the top, as you are taking a breather, turn round and (on a clear day) enjoy a panoramic view which includes the Malverns and Bredon Hill.

After crossing the stile, turn right onto a bridleway soon to go through a metal gate and continue on an enclosed path. At the end of this, pass though another gate to reach an asphalt drive, the house on the left sporting a weather vane with a fox in full flight. The drive gives way to Avenue Road (where bus travellers will find their stop) and which leads motorists straight up to the A441 where, by the Bell Inn, you turn left to walk back to your starting place.

11

West from 'Ambridge'

An excursion into mid-Worcestershire from the Archers' village to savour the peace and quiet of the tiny village of Dormston.

Distance: 7½ miles (shorter route 6½miles).
Start: On the village green in Inkberrow (GR015573)
Maps: Landranger 150; Pathfinder 996 & 997; Explorer 204 & 205.
Car Parking: Roadsides on the road leading from the village green towards the church in Inkberrow. (GR015573).
Public Transport: Bus service 350 (Redditch-Worcester) stops near the village green.
Refreshments: The Bull's Head and The Old Bull's Head in Inkberrow.

! A section of bridleway on the longer walk can be very wet and muddy so it might be preferable to follow this option in a settled dry period.

THE walk starts on the village green where a circular seat commemorates the Jubilees of 1935 and 1977. Walk up to the main road, cross it and turn right. Immediately past the village shop, fork left onto a tarmacked footpath (signposted Dormston and Stockwood) which slants upwards from the former Bethesda Chapel. When you meet a road (High House Drive), bear left onto it and walk ahead for about 100 yards. When you reach a T-junction, go left and after about 20 yards right into Tuer Way. At the end of this, go through a kissing gate, cross a grassy ride and climb over a stile which is beside a double farm gate opposite you.

Walk ahead to the left of a large barn and continue, hedge on left, to pass between houses and reach another road (Withybed Lane). Here turn left and, after about 200 yards, you reach a crossroads where you turn right into Broadclose Lane to enjoy, on clear days, good views of the Malvern ridge. Continue on this lane to Broadclose Farm. Go through its farmyard and the gate at its end, a few yards beyond which you veer left through a muddy gateway. Beyond this, bear half-right and aim for another gateway close to the far corner of the field and to the right of the rightmost of two double power posts. Having gone through the gateway, go half-left, targeting a wicket gate at the next field's far corner. Pass through this gate and enter the corner of a strip of woodland.

Now walk ahead for 20 yards or so and then turn right to cross a stile which may have been obscured from your view by hawthorn bushes. Your right-of-way then goes half-left across a field to a stile in a wire fence, beyond which you turn right onto a tractor track.

Near the banks of the nearby fishing lake, you will probably see the tall stems of teasel plants topped by their spiny seed heads which are a favourite source of food of goldfinches. The plant is so-called because its spiny heads were used to 'tease' out the fibres of wool in old tweed mills and they are still used in production of the green baize used on snooker tables.

Continue on the track until you come to a road. Cross the road and go over a stile to the right of the drive of Hill Farm House. Here you are again confronted, on clear days, which the Malvern panorama. Walk ahead down the meadow to cross a stile and, having done this, walk on to climb over another stile straight ahead of you. Now continue with a hedge on your right.

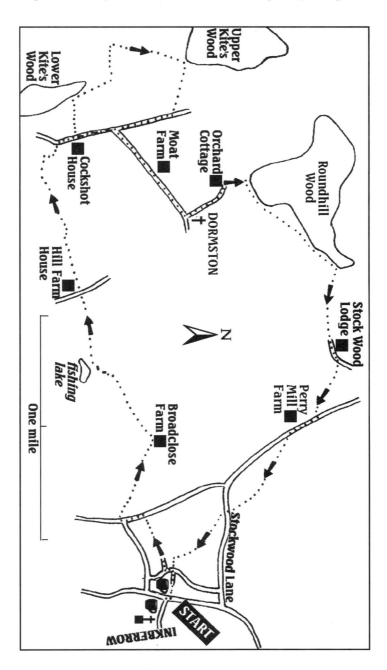

When you reach the end of this field, go through a gate on your right and, in 20 yards, go through another on your left. Walk on, again keeping the hedge on your right, to go over a stile. Still close to the hedge, you now walk across the ends of 3 narrow fields, passing through a hedge gap and over a stile (somewhat obscured by undergrowth) connecting them *en route*. At the end of the third field, the stile you need to cross is clearly visible some 30 yards to the <u>left</u> of the field's bramble-covered corner. Having negotiated it, turn right (ignoring a waymark indicating a left turn) and follow the hedge as it soon swings left and goes down a gradual slope. Near the bottom of this, climb over a stile on your right, continue down the slope and, when you reach a stream, go right to reach and cross a footbridge. Now walk up an incline to reach a road onto which you turn right.

Most of the red fruits of our autumn hedgerows, such as the hips of roses and the haws of hawthorn, are scarlet in colour. However, those of the spindle tree are different in that they are of an unusual deep pink hue and, when ripe, they split open to expose a bright orange seed which, according to Boulger's Familiar Trees, is 'one of the most daring of Nature's colour contrasts'. In late autumn, these fruits may help you to recognise several of these trees hereabouts.

Walk on for nearly 150 yards where, at Cockshot Farm and House, the two routes diverge.

*Those who are taking the **shorter route** now walk ahead along the road and, in 250 yards, following the signpost to Dormston, turn right to join the longer walk at ★ on page 56.*

Those who intend to cover the **longer route**, turn left over the stile opposite Cockshot House. With the boundary on your right, walk on, towards the trees of Lower Kite's Wood, crossing a stile on your way. On reaching the woodland, turn right over a stile. Continue over another stile and when you reach a farm gate, go through this and turn left onto an enclosed bridleway. When you reach a tall wicket gate, go through it and walk ahead. In just under 100 yards, pass through a kissing gate on your right. Now go a quarter-right across this reedy meadow to pass over a stile and plank bridge. Follow the hedge on your left for about 50 yards. At this point, it swings away to the left but you steer only slightly left to cross a stile in a wire fence which is midway between the hedge and a tree-fringed pond. Walk on and admire, in autumn, the rich variety of autumn colours in the woodland ahead.

The woodland ahead is Upper Kite's Wood so these fine birds may have been here in years past. The kite was a common British bird of prey until the eighteenth century, even scavenging in the streets of medieval London. However, it is now confined to a very few areas in Wales, though attempts to re-introduce it to England are showing success.

Cross a pair of stiles in the far right-hand corner of the field and turn right to walk down a bridleway, disturbing the occasional pheasant as you go and noticing, near its end on the right, an oak with a heavily-calloused trunk. On reaching a road, turn right and, in 500 yards, turn left into a road signposted to Dormston, here to be joined by those who used the shorter route.

★ *As you walk on, you will pass the multi-gabled, half-timbered Moat Farm built in 1663. Note the courses of tiles projecting from its walls. Nearby is a dovecote with a lantern top. Sometimes housing hundreds, even thousands, of birds, dovecotes were built to a variety of designs. Sometimes they were integral parts of other buildings but the free-standing ones were said to be sited a little way from the farmhouse because noise and smell. Pigeon meat provided an important protein source.*

Continue past Moat Farm for a further quarter of a mile where you turn left into a lane, soon to enter the graveyard of St Nicholas' Church, Dormston under an archway of holly and yews.

This old church, with a slightly tilted tower and off-vertical windows, has an ancient timbered porch and some antique oak pews. Its sundial in memory of Callow Morris and Joseph Green, churchwardens in 1841, was made by Thomas Davis of Inkberrow. He is described as a 'sciagrapher' or sundial-maker, a word derived from the Greek word 'skia' (= shadow) and 'graphe' (= writing). Churches with half-timbered towers like this and the one in neighbouring Kington are, according to Arthur Mee, known as 'Forest Churches'.

After seeing the church (and, maybe, resting on the seat on its south side), go back to the lane and turn right. Walk on up the lane for about 300 yards until you reach Orchard Cottage. About 60 yards beyond this, the surface having now deteriorated into a muddy track, turn right through a metal gate and walk ahead with woodland at your left hand. After a little over 250 yards, just beyond the woodland, the bridleway passes through a hedge. On the other side, the line of the right-of-way goes half-right across the field, aiming for the right-hand end of Roundhill Wood. However, crop obstructions may force you to turn left and walk around the perimeter, especially in winter months – hoofmarks may confirm that horse riders have also made this choice.

Church of St Nicholas, Dormston

Sundial on Dormston Church

Having reached the far corner of Roundhill Wood, turn right soon to pass an oak and two ashes and a few yards of isolated hedgerow. Continue along the line of the grubbed-up hedge to pass through a gateway and turn left. Now follow a rough track down past Stock Wood Lodge. The surface improves and, ignoring paths off to the right, continue for 100 yards where the lane bears left. About 30 yards after the bend, you join a track on the right. Follow this for about a quarter of a mile where, soon after it swings left, it joins a road opposite Chapel House. Here turn right onto the road.

For the last mile or so, you have been circling a red-brick tower on a hill near Inkberrow. You are now walking directly towards this tower which was built on the site of a World War II observation post and is, in fact, a relay station for a mobile phone company.

The footpaths from now on are not easy so there are two options.

- **Option 1** involves footpaths and is the route shown on the map. About 300 yards after joining the road, you come to a sign for Berrowsfield Farm immediately beyond which is Perry Mill Farm. Opposite these, you cross a double stile and go half-right to reach the far corner of the field. Go through a gate, walk ahead on a wired-off area for about 40 yards to pass through another gate on your right. Now go half-left up the next field where you cross another double stile. Beyond this, go half-right and, on reaching a hedge-elbow, go slightly more to the right to reach a stile. Go over this, cross the lane and negotiate the stile opposite you. Now aim half-left on a footpath which takes you up a field, then on reaching the far boundary turn right along a grassy ride for 50 yards to a stile near houses.

- **Option 2** is for those who dislike mud, who are afraid of cattle and are uneasy about crossing fields on un-reinstated paths. They should follow the road for nearly half-a-mile and fork left into Stockwood Lane. After a quarter of a mile, after going up a slope in the road, they turn right opposite a farm and go straight ahead across a field to a stile near houses.

Having made your choice and reached the stile by the houses, the two options join. Cross the stile and walk along the grassy ride for 50 yards. Here turn left over a stile and walk between houses to reach a road where you turn right. Stay on it as it swings left and, at a junction, go slightly right into High House Drive, rejoining your outward path. Slant right in front of numbers 1 and 2 Field House. On emerging onto the main road, turn right and, in a further 50 yards, cross the road to the village green where you set out earlier in the day.

12

From Anglo-Saxon beginnings in Wootton Wawen

Distance: 8½ miles.
Start: On the A3400 at the end of the lane leading to St Peter's church, Wootton Wawen (GR153633)
Maps: Pathfinder 975; Landranger 151; Explorer 220.
Car Parking: Parking is not permitted on the A3400 but space should be found on roadsides on the B4089 to Alcester.
Public Transport: Rail: Birmingham New Street to Wootton Wawen; Bus: The X50 service between Birmingham and Stratford stops at Wootton Wawen.
Refreshments: The Navigation and the Bull's Head at Wootton Wawen and the Crabmill at Preston Bagot.

Prominent in the village of Wootton Wawen, the church of St Peter, said, in the church's guidebook, to be one of Warwickshire's 'oldest, largest and structurally most noteworthy churches', is a fine landmark at which to start your walk. The Saxon Sanctuary exhibition is

Wootton Wawen Church

immediately an attractive diversion but you may choose to visit it on your return to the village.

The form of the places of worship here have evolved through many stages since a Benedictine monastery occupied this site in AD700. The guidebook traces that evolution informatively but you would be wise to delay your visit to the church until you have completed the walk.

With your back to the church, turn left and walk along the pavement, soon noticing Wootton Hall across the parkland to your left. It was built in 1687, rebuilt in the late seventeenth century and bears, on the elevation facing you, the coat-of arms of the 1st Viscount Carington. Reminded that you are 100 miles from London, you soon cross the River Alne where waterfalls foam spectacularly after heavy rain. Continue past a converted mill and, immediately past a Craft Centre, turn left into Pettiford Lane. Walk carefully up this pavement-free lane, opting for the right-hand side. After about 100 yards, having passed the

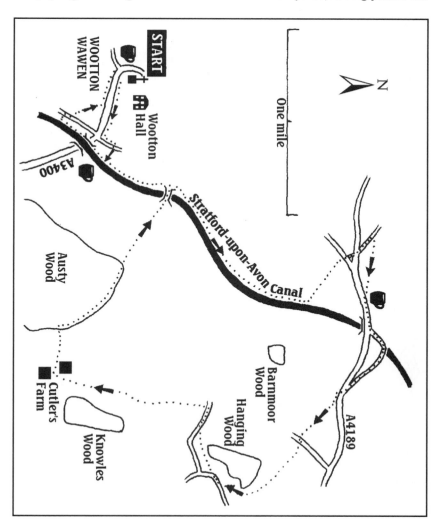

car park of the Craft Centre, turn right onto a private road to Lucy Farm, soon to reach the Stratford-upon-Avon Canal. Turn left and proceed on the towpath for about a mile and a half, enjoying the wildlife as you go.

Look out for common water birds like moorhens and mallards, the occasional heron as well as the usual blackbirds, finches and tits. You may even be fortunate enough to see the metallic-blue of a kingfisher flashing away from you. On your left, just beyond bridge 50, you will see, in the form of a fallen tree, a still-life example of nature's own work of art.

When you reach bridge 49, the patch of woodland on a knoll to your right is Barnmoor Wood and occupies the site of an ancient fort.

Many of the bridges on this canal are only about seven feet wide. Some, like this one, still have a slit through the centre that allowed the towrope of horse-drawn boats to pass through, thus speeding the progress of the narrow boats. The slit is open on only a few bridges now, many having been filled or obstructed as bridges have been repaired or strengthened.

150 yards beyond bridge 49, cross a stile on your left and traverse the nearby footbridge. Follow a clear path across rough ground and continue on the same bearing across the field, aiming for a tall oak tree at the top of the rise. At the other side of the field, join a rough track which continues up the slope. Pass through a gate beneath your target oak and continue to a lane (Pettiford Lane again). Here turn right and soon take the left fork (sign-posted Henley and Redditch) to reach, and cross with care, the Warwick Road along which some drivers are inclined to race. Enter the (un-named) lane opposite and walk on for 150 yards or so until, opposite a house with a wind-pump in its garden, climb over a stile on your right.

Go forward and walk down a meadow with the boundary on your left. At the bottom, obscured until you reach it, is a stile. Having negotiated this, go half-right down the incline in the next field, aiming just right of the Crabmill. On

Nature's work of art

reaching the road, bear left, pass the pub and a turn for Preston Bagot and, just before tall evergreens, bear left into a no-through-road – the route of the old Warwick Road prior to road-straightening. You pass the half-timbered Preston Bagot Manor and soon cross the Stratford-upon-Avon Canal again.

Continue along the old road, soon swinging right through a metal, farm gate, shortly followed by a second. Go on until you reach a third gate. Pass through this and reach the main road again. Turn left and walk along the grass verge for about 150 yards. Now, with great care cross the road at the point where, on the other side, a short track takes you to steps on the left up to a stile. After the stile, go slightly left across a field to pass through a gateway and continue, slightly left again, across the next field to climb over another stile and pass through a short patch of woodland to reach a road.

Here turn left and, after about 30 yards, turn right into a gravelled driveway immediately before a road leading to Greenfingers (Kenilworth) Ltd. Take the enclosed footpath to the left of the metal gates of Meadowside. When the path emerges onto rough ground, continue with a stream on your left until you pass on the left a well-waymarked farm gate. Here cross a tarmac road and aim slightly right across the rough ground, making for a stile beside a gate just left of a corrugated iron barn. Immediately past the barn, turn right over a stile then, in the next field, bear left and then walk diagonally to reach the field's far right-hand corner. Cross a stile by a gate and then, about 20 yards ahead, look for a stile on your left. Cross this and walk up a grassy slope to the right of wooden paddock railings to reach the top of the field.

At the top of the incline, if you need a rest, turn round and admire the view. A mile-and-a-half to the north-west, you may see Preston Bagot church perching on the hillside. You may have enjoyed marvellous views from it when it was visited on Walk 12 in Country Walks in Warwickshire and Worcestershire.

Cross one stile and then, on your right, another. Now go ahead through a spinney soon to cross another stile. Beyond this, walk ahead, again beside paddock railings, to reach a road onto which you turn right. After about 75 yards, cross a stile on the right and then go half-left across the next field to climb over a stile. As you cross it, you might ponder on the reason for the woodland on your right being called Hanging Wood!

Now bear half-right down the slope following the waymarks on posts, stiles and (finally) on a wicket gate which leads to a lane. Here turn right and continue on the lane for a little over 200 yards. At that point, and opposite Kington Cottage, turn left up a rough lane (Chestnut Rise) and, just before the gates of Chestnut Rise Farm, turn left and make your way up a narrow bridleway. Pass through a gateway and start walking down a long slope, always following the clear bridleway with, on clear days, good views south. Cutlers Farm soon comes into view.

To your left is Knowles Wood, which is what Phil Drabble has called a 'bluebell-bottomed wood'. Particularly enchanting in the bluebell season and can be visited on Walk 9. Look out, in the adjacent fields, for muntjac deer which have crept out from the sanctuary of the woodland to feed.

At Cutlers Farm, after walking past modernised farm cottages and buildings converted for various commercial uses, turn right just before the farmhouse and walk through the farmyard to pass through a gate. Now continue your walk, twisting your way up a grassy slope, keeping the boundary fairly close to your left hand. On reaching the top of the incline, bear right for about 100 yards to pass through a wicket gate. After 10 yards or so, bear right to join a bridleway which runs just within the north-west edge of Austy Wood. After an initial rise, continue down the bridleway's gradual slope, staying on it as it emerges from the wood. When you reach the Stratford-on-Avon Canal again, cross the bridge (number 51) and turn left. Now follow the towpath for about half-a-mile when you cross the aqueduct over the A3400.

This aqueduct. a major engineering feat of its time, is one of three of its type on this canal. They were built by William Whitmore between 1812 and 1816 and are constructed of cast-iron plates bolted together. This one is now designated as a Scheduled Ancient Monument. Its low-slung towpath affords a 'duck's eye view' of passing boats.

Beyond the aqueduct, continue on the towpath for about 350 yards. On reaching bridge 54, turn right and walk down a rough lane. At the next intersection, turn right and after nearly 100 yards and just after a tall evergreen hedge, pass through a wicket gate on your left and walk across a plank bridge and then through a spinney to cross a stile. Go half-left, immediately passing a nearly-garrotted horse-chestnut tree. On reaching another rough lane, bear right and, just beyond eagle-guarded gates, reach the busy A3400. Turn left and you are soon back at your starting place. The Bull's Head is close by.

The Bull's Head, Wootton Wawen

13

Windmills and Inigo Jones

This walk visits three quiet villages in south-east Warwickshire: Harbury, Chesterton and Bishops Itchington, and finds some connections with Inigo Jones

Distance: 7 miles.
Start: All Saints' Church, Harbury (GR374600).
Maps: Landranger 151; Pathfinder 998; Explorer 206.
Car Parking: Roadsides near All Saints' Church in Harbury.
Public Transport: Stagecoach bus service 64/65 from Leamington stops at Harbury. Leave the bus at Harbury Village Hall (at the far end of the village, travelling from Leamington) and opposite the Hall walk down Ivy Lane to reach the Dog Inn. Turn right here to reach the starting point at the church – or turn left to pick up the walk at the house with the 1577 inscription (end of the second sentence in the first paragraph).
Refreshments: There are, within 100 yards of the church, several public houses in Harbury.

The walk starts at the south (main) gate of All Saints' Church, Harbury, a stone-built church with a squat, red-brick tower. With your back to the church, turn right and walk down Church Street, continuing ahead when you reach the road junction, bearing slightly to the left of the house bearing a 1577 inscription and passing The Bull Ring on the left. In about 100 yards, you pass, on your right, Mill Lane in which is Harbury Windmill, now devoid of sails and converted for domestic use.

In his Bird's Eye View: the Midlands, *Vivian Bird records that, in the eighteenth century, a miller was killed here by rotating sails and, a century later, another was killed when he became entangled in the mill's machinery.*

Continuing past Mill Lane, walk on down Mill Street for a little over a quarter of a mile, noticing, as you go, the curious mixture of old and new houses, some delightfully named. Very shortly after the road narrows and begins to ascend meet a grassy area on the left. Here turn left into Farm Street and walk on to the Old New Inn.

Again according to Vivian Bird, it was in the New Inn, Harbury that farm labourers met in January 1872 to demand higher wages. Joseph Arch (from Barford in Warwickshire and later to become an MP) soon afterwards set up a national union which held its first strike in March 1872.

At the main road, turn right and, after about 100 yards, cross it carefully (you are on a blind bend here and traffic may approach at speed) and go over a stile which is at the end of a garden wall. Walk ahead with wooden palings now on your right and, at the bottom of the slope, cross a stile and short concrete bridge. Continue ahead, with the hedge now at your left, through five fields. Towards the end of the second of these, you may see, half-right, the top of the Chesterton Windmill.

The Chesterton Windmill was designed and built in 1632, possibly by Inigo Jones, as an observatory and was later converted into a windmill. It stands on six semi-circular arches and commands a panoramic view over the surrounding countryside. (Though not included on the route of this walk, its entrance is about half a mile up the road which you are about to cross.)

On reaching the road, turn right and, in 30 yards, cross to join a bridleway which slants off a quarter-right up a field. The contrast between the footpath which you have just left and the bridleway which you are now using will please those who have difficulty with stiles! At the next wicket gate (now with Chesterton Windmill in fuller view to your right), take the path which goes slightly to the left towards some abandoned cottages. As you go, your next objective, St Giles' Church, Chesterton, is in view. Pass through the wicket gate near the cottages and through a farm gate 10 yards beyond and then turn left through another wicket gate. Now aiming at the left (east) end of the church,

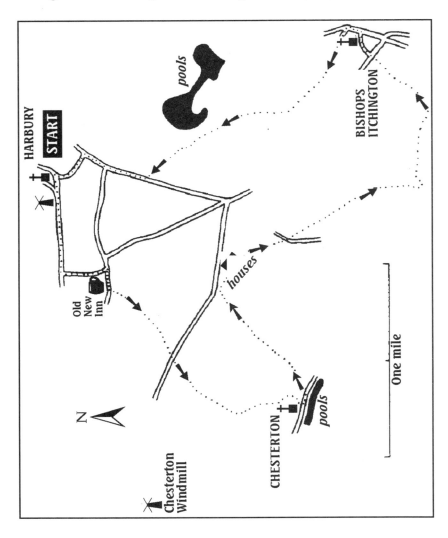

you walk diagonally down the meadow (on the footpath, not the bridleway which goes more sharply to the right) at the bottom of which you cross a stile and footbridge, which are obscured until the last minute by a large hawthorn.

The brick archway ahead of you – the Peyto Gateway – is said to be another Inigo Jones design and was built at about the same time as the Chesterton Windmill. It provided a private entrance to the church for the Peyto family from the Manor House which, until it was pulled down in 1802, stood near the abandoned cottages which you passed earlier. Further details are to be seen on a plaque on the south side of the arch.

To reach the churchyard, walk half-left up the next meadow and enter via a gate. Many churches in the area having suffered from vandalism and theft, you may well find the church to be locked but a notice in the porch proclaims that 'This community is recorded in the *Domesday Book, 1086*'. On leaving the porch, look behind you to read the legend on the sundial which exhorts you to 'See and be gone about your business', your immediate business being to walk slightly right down a path and pass through a gate to reach a lane with fish-pools ahead.

Turn left and follow the lane for about 100 yards where you cross a stile on your left and then go half-right across a field aiming for the left-hand edge of an oblong of woodland (called Coppice Moor). Cross a stile and follow the path which is perpendicular to the fence which you have just crossed. Passing just to the right of an isolated oak, you reach and cross another stile. Now slant slightly right up the slope, aiming just left of the top of a tree which is peeping over the horizon. You may choose to pause at the brow of the hill to enjoy good views over surrounding countryside. On reaching houses, turn right and follow a bridleway. Pass through a farm gate and, after about 400 yards, a wicket gate. 150 yards beyond the latter, go through a double farm gate, bear right onto a lane and, in 35 yards, fork left to re-join the bridleway (now following the Centenary Way).

At the end of a small spinney, pass through a wicket gate and continue ahead, with the boundary still on your left. Immediately after entering the second field, a stile on your left leads to the more direct route into Bishops Itchington. However, at the time of writing, it passed through a crop of oilseed rape which, though the path had been reinstated after planting, near harvest-time proved to be impenetrable. (Beware! This route is no better in winter since it involves a long, very muddy tractor track!)

Oilseed rape may be the walkers' enemy but it would also seem to be the farmers' friend. In 1998, the crop was grown on over 500 thousand hectares in the U.K. (the total area of Warwickshire is just under 200 thousand hectares), yielding over 1.5 million tonnes of seed. The oil extracted is used in food products (e.g. cooking oil, margarine and confectionary) and in manufacture of soap, detergents and paints. Rape meal, which remains after the oil has been removed from the seeds, is used for animal feed.

So, ignoring this stile, walk on for nearly half a mile. A little over 150 yards after the next gate, leave the Centenary Way and go through a wicket gate on your left. Follow a rough bridleway across a short field and then, through a hedge-gap, across the next field (swinging slightly right). Crossing a sleeper bridge and stile beneath a rather lanky ash tree, bear slightly left across the next field, aiming to the left of a patch of taller trees. (On clear days your navigation will be confirmed by a tall, slender tower on the distant horizon.)

Cross a stile and walk down the next field, keeping close to the tall hedge on your right. After climbing the stile at the bottom of the field, turn left and continue down the slope to cross a stile. Now follow the right-hand boundary through sheep pasture, the top of Bishops Itchington church tower being just visible above trees ahead. On reaching a road, cross it and go into Manor Road opposite and follow this as it soon curves right to join the main road (B4451) through Bishop's Itchington.

Turn left and, 100 yards beyond the church, leave the main road and walk up Church Close (signed Church Close leading to Mount Pleasant). When this angles off to the right, your (tarmac) path continues ahead to the left of houses, soon crossing a road. After the houses, walk on, with the fence at your left hand, through two fields – during your passage through the second of which you may see ahead (and a little to the right) the sail-less windmill that you passed earlier in Harbury. The path goes half-right across a third field and, after crossing a stile in its far corner, you turn left and follow the hedge until, some 70 yards before that field's end, you slant off to the right passing near to the edge of deep, water-filled quarries, formerly used by cement manufacturers.

The hedge beside which you have just walked will, in summer and early autumn, have been festooned with goosegrass or cleavers. If you have followed the route at that time of year, you socks may well be unwitting agents of that plant's dispersal, its fruits being covered with hooked prickles. Take care when you get home for, as Rev. C A Johns confirmed in his Flowers of the Field *(1920), goosegrass is 'an objectionable weed in gardens'.*

A double stile and plank bridge lead to the next field down which you walk to a bridge and a gate. After this, the path goes slightly right to another stile/bridge complex in the fence. Cross this and turn left to walk beside the hedge for about 300 yards where you turn right onto a busy road. Soon after the 40 m.p.h. sign, cross the road and, now making use of pavements, continue until you reach Vicarage Lane. Turn left into this and you soon reach Harbury church where your walk began.

14

A Triangular Walk from Southam

This slightly longer walk visits the delightful village of Napton-on-the-Hill with its prominent windmill.

Distance: 10 miles. A much shorter version, concentrating on Napton, starts and ends at the Bridge pub and covers 2 miles. For the shorter walk start reading from ★ on page 71.
Start: High Street, Southam (GR419618).
Maps: Landranger 151; Pathfinder 977; Explorer 222.
Car Parking: Free car-park in Wood Street, Southam, well-signposted off the main street. (From the car park, turn right and walk up to the main street and then turn left into High Street, soon to reach the start.).
Public Transport: Bus services 63 and 65, from Leamington pass through Southam.
Refreshments: The Bridge (by Oxford Canal), The Crown Inn (in Napton village), the Barley Mow (in Stockton) and various establishments in Southam, including the Old Mint House.

THE walk starts outside Lloyds TSB Bank in High Street, the main street through Southam. Go round the corner into Daventry Street, staying on this as it joins Daventry Road and twists its way down to a roundabout. Using the refuge to the left of this roundabout, cross the Southam by-pass (A423) and then go straight ahead, using the footpath on the left of the A425 Daventry Road. After 75 yards turn left onto a bridleway, walking on tarmac between palings for about 30 yards. At this point, just before evergreen trees, turn off to the right soon to pass through a metal, wicket gate.

You will notice unusual blue waymarks here and you will see more of them throughout this walk. They mark the Blue Lias Rings, a series of circular walks in the area. The name is derived from the lias clay deposits which have made this an important area for cement manufacture. This clay is fossil-rich – hence the ammonite on the waymarks.

The Blue Lias Rings waymark

Your path, initially close to the River Stowe, soon leads you behind the Southam Zoological Gardens where you might see varieties of domestic fowl. Immediately beyond the zoo, you enter a large field. Walk straight ahead across this, Napton windmill coming into view, half-right, as you go. After the next gate, walk on with the tall hedge on your left for about 350 yards. When you have walked between palings whilst crossing a stream, you veer a third-left across the next field, aiming for a signpost which you will be able to spot on the horizon some 200 yards away. After the signpost, proceed with a hedge again on your left until you reach another wicket gate.

This is the ninth (and last) gate of this design that you have passed through on this walk. Various means have been devised to allow rights-of-way to make stock-proof crossings over field boundaries. Not all of them are convenient for walkers, some being extremely hazardous! These gates are ideal, even being rider-friendly in that they have vertical latch-levers.

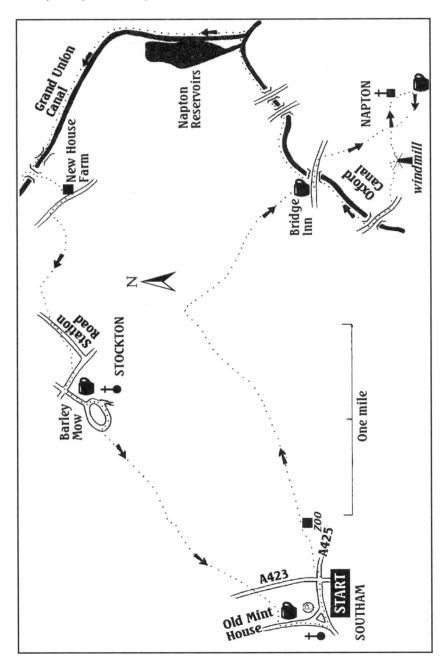

Having passed through the gate, you go slightly left across the next field for 75 yards to pass through a hedge gap. Walk on, hedge on left through (at the time of writing) two fields – but be aware that hedge-removal might ultimately make this into one, very large plot. After just over a quarter of a mile, having crossed a drainage ditch, you swing right to reach and cross a wide footbridge. After 70 yards or so, you pass through a farm gate and go forward along the field edge. At the end of this field, you leave the bridleway and turn *right* to walk beside a barbed wire fence and hedge.

When you reach the corner of the field, cross a stile (your first on the walk thus far!) and then go *slightly* left across the next field to pass through a waymarked hedge gap. You are now in a large field which has five electricity posts standing in it (originally two fields with some parts of a boundary hedge remaining). Your next objective is a footbridge which lies 250 yards beyond the middle post, 20 yards to the left of a pair of oaks. (If the path across this field has not been reinstated, you may decide to use tractor tracks to get across, adjusting when you reach the other side.) Having crossed the bridge and its stile, go forward with a wire fence on your right and continue to reach a road. Here turn left to walk in front of The Bridge pub.

★ *The short route begins here.*

Cross the A425 at the canal bridge where visibility is at its best. Having done this, turn left and walk for nearly 150 yards at which point you reach a road to an industrial estate. Here, turn right off the A425 and cross the waymarked stile ahead of you. Walk up two sloping fields with the hedge on your right. After crossing a stile at the end of the second field, bear half-left across pronounced ridge-and-furrow to climb over another stile overhung by hawthorns. Now walk straight ahead for 75 yards across a sheep pasture to reach a lane by a stile.

On the far side of the stile, you will see a notice adjuring you to follow the Country Code – this, unusually written in Welsh as well as English! (It was, apparently, put there by Mr Crick, joint-owner of the nearby Church Leyes Farm.)

Turn left to walk along a rough track to St. Lawrence's Church, Napton.

Few churches command such a commanding position as this. Saint Lawrence's is a light, airy church and merits inspection. The churchyard, and indeed the whole village, is well-equipped with seats from which one can enjoy spectacular views – allegedly, on clear days, of seven counties.

From the church's south door, walk down the gravel path between pollarded lime trees and continue downwards past a graveyard extension in which primroses are abundant in spring. A tarmac path leads steeply down towards the village. When you reach a small triangle of grass, you have two choices, depending on your degree of thirst! You can either carry on down to the Crown Inn or you can turn right to walk past a converted 1867 Baptist chapel and soon branch right into Mill Road. Continue on this is it slopes upwards, *en route* bearing left in front of the stile bearing the bilingual country code. About 120 yards after this stile, you reach roadside seats.

These seats are close to the site of an observer post from which the many nights of the Coventry blitz were witnessed in 1940. Mr Andy Bean, the local footpaths officer, remembers that, as a child at that time, he was taken into the underground bunker below the single-storey look-out post. Passers-by are invited to remember those people who, though not members of the armed forces, played such an important part in securing our freedom during World War II.

Continue up the road to the windmill which, though complete with sails, is now converted to domestic use. Immediately before the windmill, take the footpath on the right and, soon after a stile, begin to curve your way down the slope, parts of which are steep and muddy, following waymarks and keeping a fence on your right. When the gradient slackens, swing left to walk with a wire-topped fence on your right beyond which are abandoned clay pits which served a now-defunct brickworks. Having passed huge boulders, continue onwards to reach a red-brick house, keeping the fence on your right. Turn right onto the road and, immediately past the canal bridge, turn right to join the towpath of the Oxford Canal.

Construction of the Oxford Canal started, under the supervision of James Brindley who was its chief engineer, near Coventry in 1769 and reached Oxford in 1789, to be officially opened the following year. Previously Oxford's coal had come from Newcastle by sea and the River Thames. The cost of coal is said to have decreased dramatically within days of the opening of this canal!

Now turn left and walk away from the bridge for about a mile. (*If you are walking the short loop leave the towpath after the first bridge, having reached the Bridge pub again.*) On the longer route, having gone under a third bridge and passed the Napton Marina, walk on for about a quarter of a mile to reach and cross a footbridge. Beyond this bear right and then execute a right-hand hairpin to join the towpath of the Grand Union Canal which leads you under the bridge. Now walk ahead on the grassy towpath.

On your left as you approach the locks at Calcutt, you will see the Napton Reservoirs. These are feeder reservoirs for the two canals and now support large numbers of water birds.

Beyond the locks, you will see another large boat mooring and you then continue on the towpath, passing the Ventnor Farm Marina and walking between the supports of a disused railway bridge. Shortly after this, you walk under a footbridge and, 10 yards beyond it, leave the towpath through a gap, turn right onto a road and, in a further 10 yards, turn right again to cross over the footbridge. Continue straight ahead on an enclosed bridleway and, having passed through a stout, metal gate, continue on the same heading, passing New House Farm to reach a road. Here you turn right and, with care, stay on the road for about 200 yards at which point you turn left off the road and walk along a drive, the first part of which is tarmacked .

Immediately beyond a clump of evergreens, cross a stile on your right and then go a third-left across the field, in the direction of a cement factory chimney on the horizon. Having negotiated another stile, go ahead, hedge at your right hand, through two fields. In the third field, go half-left, targeting a gate in its far corner. (Crop obstruction may make a direct line to the gate impossible, but tractor tracks could then be used.) On reaching Station Road, turn left.

On your right, metal security fencing surrounds a disused quarry, one of several hereabouts, from which clay was extracted to feed the cement factories.

At the end of security fence, enter a field by way of a stile and walk, parallel to the road, with the hedge on your left, the tower of Stockton church being ahead of you. Pass through a hedge gap to enter a sports ground. Your right of way goes a third-right across this, but you will, no doubt, defer to any match which is in progress at the time by steering to its left! On reaching the hedge at the far side, turn right to walk beside it, leaving the sports ground through its main gate. Cross Napton Road and turn right and walk on the pavement soon to turn into Post Office Lane. At a T-junction, turn left to walk in front of the Barley Mow to reach Stockton church.

If you are fortunate, the Church of Saint Michael and All Angels will not be padlocked. Enter through the main door (unusually, on the north side) and, at the top of the north aisle, you will find a war memorial on which are the names of 130 people who served in World War I (of whom thirty-one died) and those of eight who lost their lives in the 1939-45 conflict. This is surrounded by the Union flag and those of Belgium, Canada, France, the USA and the British Legion.

Leave the churchyard by its north-west gate (nearest the Barley Mow) and walk into the second road on your left (*not* Rectory Close) and curve your way round Church Street and Saint Michael's Crescent for about 300 yards until you come to a footpath which goes off *sharply* to the left leading to the Stockton Children's Playing Fields. Join this and, keeping to the field's right-hand margin, cross over a stile and follow the field edge for 45 yards where you veer slightly right by a stile. Now continue on your former heading with the field edge now on your left, the fifteenth century spire of Southam church coming into view straight ahead.

Cross a farm lane and continue slightly right across the next field to pass through a hedge gap. Now go half-left, pass through a hedge on a plank bridge and maintain the same heading across the next field. On reaching a hedge-corner, walk on with the hedge on your right. Cross a stile and continue across the corner of the field soon to reach another hedge and continue on its left. After nearly 150 yards, this hedge bends off to the right but you continue straight ahead, soon passing to the right of an isolated clump of hawthorn.

Go through a hedge gap and continue, aiming slightly to the left of the electricity post which lies ahead of you. Just beyond the post, continue to the left of a hedge, pass through another hedge gap and then go straight ahead across the next field. After this, cross the bypass, walk up the short, tarmacked drive opposite, pass through a kissing gate and take the path ahead of you, ignoring those to right and left. Continue on this path which winds its way between houses, beside a playing field and past a school, finally to emerge onto Coventry Road. Here you turn left to walk back into Southam.

You will see, on your left, the Old Mint House. It is said that, after the Battle of Edgehill in 1642, Charles I required his local nobles to surrender their silver here for it to be melted down and minted into coins with which his surviving soldiers were paid. The grooves on the doorposts are said to have been made by these soldiers sharpening their swords while awaiting payment!

15

Stock Green, Huddington and Himbleton

This walk, through quiet countryside which is studded with patches of woodland, can afford good distant views.

Distance: 7½ miles.
Start: Stock Green at the signpost where Cockshot Lane (leading to Dormston and Flyford Flavell) leaves the main road through the village (GR977585).
Maps: Landranger 150; Pathfinder 996; Explorer 204.
Car Parking: Roadside on Cockshot Lane in Stock Green (signposted Dormston and Flyford Flavell). It is suggested that you park 100 yards or so from its north end where the lane widens appreciably.
Public Transport: Bus service 353 Droitwich/Worcester (limited service) calls at Stock Green. Leave the bus at Cockshot Lane.
Refreshments: Galton Arms, Himbleton.

! Be prepared for mud if the walk is attempted after heavy rain.

WITH your back to the signpost turn right and, walk about 15 yards westwards along the main road. On the right, cross a plank bridge, walk between houses, cross over a stile and then go forward with the field boundary at your right hand. Having passed through a farm gate, you will see, slightly to the left across the next field, a row of five trees. Your next objective is a footbridge which lies between the second and third tree from the left. After this, go slightly left across the next field to cross another footbridge. Beyond this, you turn left and walk beside the hedge for nearly 200 yards to cross a stile and plank bridge in the field's corner (having ignored the waymarked gate 30 yards before it on the left). You now aim up a gentle incline towards the red-brick farmhouse of Lower Hollowfields Farm. In front of the house is a clipped hedge. When you reach this, turn left and walk along the edge of the field, passing to the left of a barn *en route*.

Probably due to modern agricultural techniques, the skylark is now one of our seriously-endangered species. You may be fortunate, in spring and early summer, to be serenaded in this area by these marvellous songsters.

On reaching the corner of Little High Wood, turn left to walk along its eastern edge. At its next corner, continue straight ahead for about 70 yards. On reaching a young oak, turn left and walk for a further 70 yards where you turn right to walk down beside Digging Wood. Continue straight ahead beyond the wood, aiming for a footbridge which lies in front of a tall hedge. Having crossed this and the stile beyond it, you enter a meadow which, in spring is bedecked with cowslips, later supporting a colourful flora including buttercups, yellow rattle and clover.

Meadows like this one are becoming rare in this country. Ancient meadows have been ploughed up and uniformly re-seeded with rye-grass which, though nutritive for livestock, destroys the botanical diversity which contributes so much to the attractiveness of the countryside.

At the far side of this meadow, you reach a road onto which you turn right and begin to walk towards the village of Earl's Common. After nearly 250 yards, turn left onto a drive. (For the next hundred yards or so, you are on the Wychavon Way which goes from the River Severn at Holt Fleet to the Cotswolds at Winchcombe.) Just before a house, cross a stile on your right and follow the hedge as it curves slightly left ahead of you. After crossing another stile, bear very slightly right across a reedy meadow, walking between woodland and a willow-fringed pool. At the corner of the wood, just beyond a metal, wicket gate, go half-left and walk in the direction of tall poplar trees in the middle distance.

Cross a stile at the edge of Hornhill Wood (which, in spring, is carpeted with primroses) and follow its margin until you reach a farm gate which accesses the wood. Here, veer off half-left across the field and, having passed the remnants of a brick bridge halfway across, use a plank bridge to ford a thin stream and climb over the stile beyond it. Now go forward for about 400 yards, following the field margin on your left, to reach a lane. (At the top of the slope you may, on clear days just to the left of a water tower, have a distant glimpse of Titterstone Clee crowned with its white radar dome.)

Cross the lane and the adjacent Shell Brook and, by way of a second footbridge and a kissing gate, enter the graveyard of the Church of Saint Mary Magdalene, Himbleton. Immediately inside the graveyard, on your right you will see a memorial to Sir Douglas Galton and, on the church tower, is a

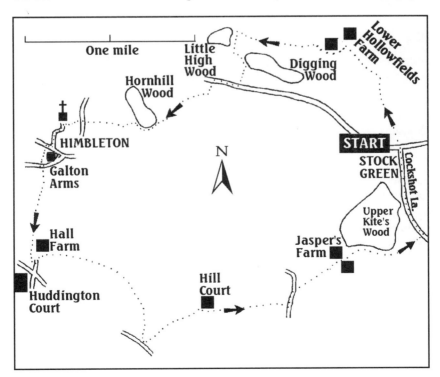

reminder that, in 1910, members of the Galton family were responsible for the provision of the clock. You will see the heraldic arms of the family on the pub sign in the village.

The 4000 oak shingles with which the tower is clad were installed in 1893. Many of these are now splitting, twisting and falling off. In 2000, a major fund-raising effort was mounted to raise the considerable sum of money required for their replacement. Contributions from passing walkers would be welcomed!

Himbleton Church

After leaving the churchyard via the lych gate, turn left and follow a lane as it passes converted farm buildings and curves right to join another lane. Here you turn left and walk down to a T-junction where you turn right and, in 80 yards, reach the Galton Arms. Immediately beyond the pub, turn left and walk along the right-hand margin of its car park at the end of which you enter an enclosed path.

After passing delightful topiary in the garden of the black-and-white Brook House, you reach another lane. Turn left and, in 100 yards, cross a stile on your right and continue on a path between an evergreen hedge and Shell Brook, the banks of which are, in summer, covered with comfrey. (The line between the stile and this point is a diversion from the right of way which, at the time of writing, goes through the garden of the adjacent house. Should an application for this diversion to be made official *not* succeed then the line will doubtless revert to the garden.)When the hedge ends, another stile leads you into a field.

Your next stile lies slightly right across this field. (Due to crop obstruction, you may be obliged to walk around the left-hand margin of the field to reach this barrier.) Having climbed over this stile, walk ahead for nearly 20 yards, cross a footbridge and then walk straight across the next field, aiming a few yards to the right of the second power post from the left that can be seen ahead. A plank bridge and pair of stiles give access to the next field along the left-hand margin of which you walk until, having passed Hall Farm on your left, you cross two stiles immediately before black-and-white cottages. After the second stile you veer left into a lane.

For those who have not visited Huddington Court (included on Walk 16 of More Country Walks), a diversion is well-worthwhile here. To do this, turn right on reaching the lane and walk ahead. Immediately after an old cottage, you cross a road to pass through wrought-iron gates and, after about 80 yards, turn right between clipped yews and then go left across a lawn to reach Saint James' Church, Huddington, admiring the Court as you go. Now, retrace your steps and continue to Hall Farm.

If you did not divert to Huddington Court, turn *left* on reaching the lane and walk along to Hall Farm. Just before the farmhouse, veer right to walk through the farmyard. After passing through three metal gates, go ahead across the field to another one, cross Bow Brook and continue, boundary to the left, for a little over 500 yards. (On days of good visibility, you will have, over your right shoulder, a distant view of the Malvern ridge.) At the end of the second field, climb over an easily missed stile and turn right onto a bridleway which, particularly in its early stages, can be exceptionally muddy in winter and at other times after heavy rain.

After about 400 yards, look out on your left for a dejected-looking wind pump with rusty, twisted sails. At this point, on the horizon on your right, you might see Abberley Hill and Woodbury Hill with Abberley Tower between them.

Continue on the bridleway until, having gone through a metal gate, you approach a road. Just before a second gate, cross a stile on your left and walk through a spinney to reach and cross another stile. Now go half-right for 100 yards across the next field aiming for a gateway. Go through the gateway and continue, with the hedge on your left with, a mile away to your right, the tower of Grafton Flyford church. After about 100 yards, you come to a dog-leg. After another 50 yards you reach a large oak tree and, 50 yards beyond this, you will see, in the hedge, a sad remnant of the English countryside.

Decomposing in its final resting place, you will see a wooden, five-barred gate. Now necessarily replaced by the metal variety which can be made much wider to accommodate the larger machinery used in modern agriculture, such gates as this are often to be seen serving a useful purpose filling hedge gaps.

Walk ahead, soon to pass through a farm gate (of the metal variety) and notice, on the horizon to your right, the great mass of Bredon Hill (visited on Walk 21). Continue up a slope to pass in front of the timber-framed farmhouse of Hill Court, some of its vertical and horizontal lines being distinctly wayward. Immediately past the house, *do not* go through the gate into the farmyard but go over the stile which is 10 yards to its right. Continue across the next field, in front of the farm buildings, to cross a stile bearing the legend 'Landowners welcome caring walkers'. Continue ahead, the boundary still on your left, through two more fields and then, ignoring a stile on the left, through another field which is divided, by wire fences, into three narrower sections, still keeping the boundary on your left. An enclosed path now leads you to a road onto which you turn left. After just over 100 yards, turn right onto a rough lane which, after 30 yards, veers left and leads towards Jasper's Farm.

One might wonder whether the man who originally farmed here was called Jasper. However, according to the present occupiers, that name does not appear in the deeds of the farm which go back to the 1700s. As you pass, notice the millstone propped in a stone trough in front of the farmhouse.

Continue beyond the farmhouse and, just beyond a couple of old railway wagons (the cargo of one of which, apparently, was fruit), go through a metal, wicket gate and then go forward through a farm gate. Soon after crossing a wide footbridge, swing right to pass through another wicket gate. The bridleway continues straight ahead just inside the southern margin of Upper Kite's Wood. However, since it is often near-impassable due to mud, you may find the path just to its left rather more hospitable.

A possible explanation of the origin of the name Upper Kite's Wood was given on page 56 of Walk 11. A less romantic interpretation could be that years ago any large bird of prey may have been classed as a kite.

At the end of the wood, the bridleway goes on ahead but you cross a stile on the *left.* (Those who have used the longer option of Walk 11 in this book will recognise this spot having crossed the stile on the right and walked on down the bridleway towards Dormston.) Climb over the stile on the left and go a third-right across two wet meadows. As you pass through the line of trees that separates the two, you will see your next objective – a metal gate – some 100 yards to the right of a thatched house. On reaching the road, turn left and continue on the road for a little over half a mile back to your starting point.

16

A Round Trip from Feckenham

A pleasant walk, mainly on fieldpaths, visiting two delightful Worcestershire villages.

Distance: 5½ miles.
Start: The Square, Feckenham (GR 010616)
Maps: Landranger 150; Pathfinder 974 & 975, Explorer 204/220.
Car Parking: There is a free car park in Feckenham on the west side of High Street about 250 yards from the B4090 (GR 009615). To reach the starting point, go back to High Street, turn left and walk for about 100 yards.
Public Transport: Nothing suitable to Feckenham. Nearest bus service (service 70 from Redditch) will take you to Astwood Bank, adding another 4 miles to the walk. For details see the box on page 80.
Refreshments: The Lygon Arms and the Rose and Crown, both in Feckenham, and the Red Lion (halfway round the walk).

! There are several short sections of this walk that can get very muddy in bad weather. A dry settled period would be the best time for following it.

THE walk starts at The Square in Feckenham which is on High Street, about 350 yards from the B4090, and adjacent to the church (which was visited on Walk 16 in *Country Walks*). Walk away from High Street soon to join Mill Lane. Walk on along this past the Ebenezer Chapel (built in 1861 but now converted for domestic use) and the village cricket ground. At the end of the gravel-surfaced section, veer to the right of The Old Mill House, pass a redundant footbridge, go through a wicket gate and use another footbridge to walk over Bow Brook.

Now walk ahead up a bridleway, the surface of which is often very muddy. After about 100 yards reach a cross-paths with a fine, metal direction post. Here turn sharp left and after about 50 yards turn right over a stile (opposite what appears to be an extremely steep and difficult short cut up from your previous path). Go straight ahead over the next field and, staying on the same line, cross a stile to continue with a hedge on your right. On clear days, you will have good views of Bredon Hill 14 miles to the south and of the Malverns 20 miles to the south-west.

After crossing two further stiles you reach a lane (Berrowhill Lane). Cross this and go through the gate opposite to enter a field. At the bottom of the slope ahead, you will see, just to the right of pools and a tennis court, two gateways. Go through the one on the right and then walk ahead with a hedge on the left through two more gateways fairly soon afterwards. Having passed through the second of these, immediately turn right to walk up a grassy incline with the hedge on your right. Go through the gateway ahead and then fork quarter-left to reach a pond, then go half-left up the hill, aiming towards the left of an area of bushes ahead. When you reach the top of the ridge, go forward to walk to the trig point on Berrow Hill.

Now at an altitude of 357 feet and having completed your day's climbing, you may wish to regain your breath and enjoy the views. To the west you have fairly flat land stretching into Warwickshire, to the south are the Cotswolds and to the more-distant west the hills of Shropshire and Wales. The Abberley Hills (with Abberley Tower between them) and the Malverns, not in view from the trig point, soon appear as you move on, with, closer at hand, Hanbury church in its commanding position slightly north of west.

When you are ready to move on, continue your line forward to cross a stile into woodland and then begin a sometimes slippery descent aided by wooden

Bus Travel

Leave the bus in Avenue Road, Astwood Bank and walk back along the road to where it swings to the right opposite Gorsey Close. Walk down Doe Bank Drive (alongside No. 74, Avenue Road) until it veers right to Doe Bank House. Cross a stile beside a green gate and follow a bridleway, then go through a gate into a field. Walk with a hedge on your left and cross a stile. Keeping to the same heading descend towards Astwood Farm. Go through a gate to the right of farm buildings and at a green silo bear right onto a concrete drive and continue on this to reach Astwood Lane.

Turn left and walk very carefully along this narrow and twisting road for a about half a mile, then look out for an easily missed finger post (Public Footpath Feckenham) on the left. Here cross a stile and follow a path to the right of an earth bank. Go through a gate, turn left along tarmac, then very shortly right up brick steps to follow another Feckenham signpost, keeping a hedge and railings on your left. Cross a lane and keeping to the left-hand hedge reach a cross a stile. Now go forward up an incline aiming about 20 yards to the right of a horse chestnut tree and going through a hedge gap midway along the facing hedge.

Walk with a hedge on your right and almost at the end of the field cross a stile, now walking with the hedge on left. The hedge is soon followed by a brick wall which leads you to the High Street where you turn left to reach the start of the walk.

Return

30 yards to the left of the Rose and Crown turn right, signed Astwood Bank, to reach a grassy area. With the field boundary on the right cross a stile, then another to walk now with the hedge on your left. Go through a hedge gap and continue forward to cross another stile, now walking with a hedge on the right. Via stiles cross tarmac and now walk with the hedge and field on your right. Descend steps, turn left, then right through a gate just before reaching the road.

Walk with the hedge on the left, cross a stile and turn right along the road. Reaching the entrance to Astwood Farm turn right along the concrete driveway, then at the green hopper go left through a gate. With a fence on the right continue via a stile, a gate and another stile to then turn right along tarmac to return to the bus stop.

staircases. When you reach the bottom of the slope, you enter an open field to bear half-left targeting a stile which soon comes into view in the field's corner, at the end of a garden protected by barbed wire.

Cross this stile and, almost immediately, pass through a gate on your left. After walking to the left of a pool, make for the far right-hand corner of this meadow where you cross another stile. Now follow the woodland margin as it swings left and, when you reach a stile, cross it and turn right onto an enclosed bridleway. After about a quarter of a mile, you reach a lane (the delightfully-named Flying Horse Lane) onto which you turn left to walk up to the main road (B4090).

This is The Salt Way and salt – then a precious commodity – was conveyed along it from Droitwich (called by the Romans Salinae) to Stratford from where it could be shipped to Bristol for further distribution, the River Avon being navigable all the way in those days.

Cross the road with care and, slightly to your left, climb over a stile (having, if required, visited The Red Lion pub which is adjacent). The field which you enter is often very marshy, the worst area being that near the road. However, this can be largely avoided by walking very close to the hedge on your right. Pick your way between the wet areas in this long, narrow field, passing to the left of an electricity post, to reach a stile at the far end. Having crossed this and the double one straight ahead, aim for a gateway at the right-hand corner of the next field

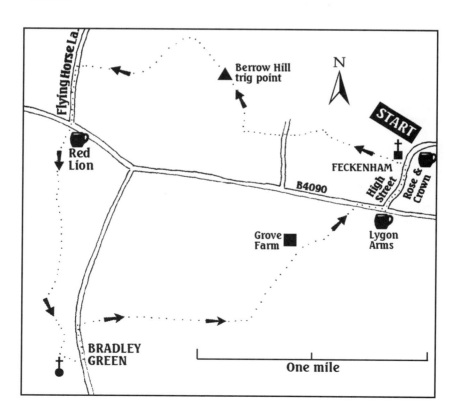

Now go quarter-left to find and cross a pair of stiles near the middle of the hedge ahead of you. (N.B. Do not cross the stile near the field's corner.) Now go straight ahead to cross a stile beneath a willow opposite you and continue with the boundary on your left, crossing three more stiles *en route*. Walk forward across the next meadow, soon to reach a hedge elbow. On reaching this, continue, on the same heading, again with the hedge at your left hand to reach and cross a stile. Here you cross a green lane to climb the stile opposite. Now bear left and follow the hedge until, having crossed a tarmac drive, you pass through a kissing gate.

This is one of a number of such gates recently installed by members of the local community to replace stiles, thus providing easy access on their Millennium Walk.

Now bear to the left of the church and its adjoining trees, cross a ditch, pass through another kissing gate and its plank bridge and then walk to Bradley Green church.

You are welcomed to the graveyard of St John the Baptist's Church with a biblical request to deter litter-droppers (although its source in the Book of Nehemiah is open to question!). Inside, the circular, stained-glass window at the west end includes eighteen regimental badges of men from the village who fought in World War 1.

Leave the churchyard through the gate at which you entered and bear half-right up a rough driveway. When you reach a road, turn left and walk on for a little over 200 yards where, just beyond Lower Beanhall Farm and opposite the white-painted Orchard Cottage, pass through a wicket gate. Now walk straight ahead across a sparse orchard and go through another wicket gate at the other end. Now bear slightly left as you walk down the next field to cross a stile and footbridge near its left-hand corner.

Negotiate another stile and plank bridge 40 yards ahead, ducking your head to avoid an overhanging willow branch. Now walk across the next field initially following the boundary hedge until this bears left, then going forward to cross a metal hurdle stile (beside the remains of an ancient wooden stile) some 20 yards from the field's left-hand corner. Walk on and, at the end of a small patch of woodland, climb a stile on your left and then resume your former bearing, now with the hedge at your right hand. At the bottom of this field, cross a footbridge and veer very slightly left to walk across a large, L-shaped field. At the far side, cross a stile 15 yards to the left of a heavily-waymarked gateway. (It boasted eight waymarks on the author's last visit!)

Now turn two-thirds-left, your next stile being in line with a green barn. Having climbed over this, continue on the same heading to pass through a gateway, 35 yards beyond which you have to negotiate an awkward, double stile on your right. This barrier behind you, walk across a paddock aiming to the left of a converted wooden barn, crossing a stile halfway along a wire fence. Now go straight across the next paddock with newly-planted trees on your left to go over a stile at its far side. Walk up a slope and through a gate to the left of Grove Farm's green barn.

Passing through the farmyard ahead, you soon reach a large hedge-gap. Your path goes across the next field and you need to aim about 70 yards to the right of the electricity post of the field's brow. (If the field is cropped and you are unable to walk across it, turn right to walk around the perimeter or along the adjoining farm lane.) On reaching two posts, one of which is waymarked, bordering a rough lane, look for a metal footbridge which may be obscured behind thick bushes. Having located this bridge and crossed Bow Brook again, turn half-left to walk across a pasture to reach a stile in front of tall evergreens. Cross this and go half-right to pass through a gate and walk to the right of a house with a candle-shaped chimney. When you reach a road, which is The Salt Way again, cross it and turn right. At the Lygon Arms, turn left into High Street and walk past a delightful variety of old houses soon to reach your starting place.

17

Alcester, a Dovecote and a Folly

A walk from a fine old Warwickshire township.

Distance: 7½ miles.
Start: By the metal gates near the west (tower) end of the church of Saint Nicholas, Alcester (GR090575).
Maps: Landranger 150; Pathfinder 997; Explorer 205.
Car Parking: Free car parks near Alcester town centre.
Public Transport: Bus service 146/176 (Birmingham/Evesham) to Alcester.
Refreshments: The Fish Inn at Wixford and numerous facilities in Alcester.

O N your left as you face the gates of Saint Nicholas is the narrow High Street. Walk along this as it passes the west end of the church soon reaching and going to the left of the War Memorial Town Hall.

This magnificent building is steeped in history. Its lower part was built in about 1620, an upper storey with a fine hammerbeam roof being constructed about 20 years later. Begun as an open market, the building's use changed over the years via a magistrates' court (complete with its lock-up, the door of which is detached, but still intact) to today's much-used meeting-place.

After the Town Hall, continue along Henley Street, soon passing the listed No. 19, Cruck House which, built in about 1385, is Alcester's oldest house. At the end of Henley Street, cross School Road and, after making your first acquaintance with the River Arrow, begin a three-quarter mile walk out of

Alcester Town Hall

Alcester up the gently-sloping Kinwarton Road. Near the top of the rise, you pass the entrance to Alcester High School. 300 yards beyond this, you turn right through a farm gate into a field immediately before a red-brick house. Your next stile is across the field, slightly to the left of a cottage (The Shepherd's Cottage) which is overshadowed by a large oak tree. Having crossed the stile turn left and, bearing right to pass Glebe Farm, you soon reach the church of Saint Mary the Virgin, Kinwarton which dates from 1291. Beyond the church, you will see the dovecote.

Described by Arthur Mee as 'one of the finest round dovecotes in Warwickshire', this sixteenth century building with a four foot high doorway is in the safe hands of the National Trust. Still within is its potence, a rotating ladder which gives access to the nests.

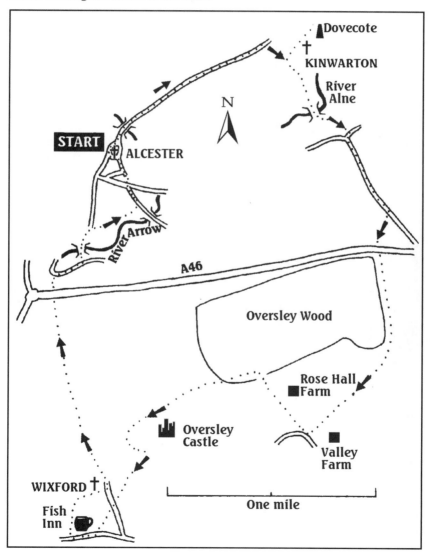

Now retrace your steps past the church and Glebe Farm until, in front of the Shepherd's Cottage, you turn left down a lane which soon degenerates into a rough track. At the end of the track, cross a stile beside a farm gate and walk straight across the next field, the River Alne initially being a few paces away to your left. As you approach the footbridge at the end of the field, you may notice Hoo Mill on the left.

The Mill, built early in the nineteenth century, is shrouded by alders and willows which, in winter sunshine, provide rich chestnut and burgundy colours. In the graveyard of Haselor church (visited on Walk 18 in More Country Walks)*, an old millstone acts as a memorial to two former residents of Hoo Mill.*

The Kinwarton Dovecote

Having crossed the footbridge, continue on an enclosed path soon passing a hollow, pollarded ash tree and, a few yards further on, a well-shaped copper beech. Just beyond this, you join a lane and continue on it for about 200 yards. On reaching a T-junction, you turn right for a few paces and then cautiously cross a busy road which carries traffic – often at high speed – in and out of Alcester. When you reach the other side, turn left and, using the grass verge, walk for nearly half-a-mile at which point, having completed the main part of the day's road-work, you turn right into a narrow lane, here joining the Arden Way.

Soon after passing the premises of a water company, you walk beneath the A46 and bear left over a stile beside a wide, farm gate. Now bear right to continue on a rough track which runs to the left of Oversley Wood. Continue hugging the wood's edge until, passing through a metal, wicket gate, you leave Oversley Wood behind, to meet it again later. Now walk ahead with a stream and hedge at your left hand. After about 300 yards, you are faced with a farm gate. Pass through this (and over the culverted stream) and continue, now with stream and hedge on your right. As you proceed, the village coming into view on the brow of the hill a mile or so to your left is Ardens Grafton (also visited on Walk 18 of *More Country Walks*).

Having passed through the farmyard of Valley Farm, you reach a road onto which you turn right and, in a few yards, veer right onto a rough lane which is a private drive. Walk up the slope and, having passed to the left of the modernised Rose Hall Farm, continue for 150 yards where you again reach Oversley Wood. Here, turn left and walk on a path just within the southern boundary of the wood for 350 yards. Your path emerges from the wood by a big oak tree. Ignoring a path to your right, go forward along a track which is surrounded by tall hedges. Soon after leaving this avenue ahead, on a hilltop, Ragley Hall comes into view and, half-left, the top of the white-painted tower of Oversley Castle.

According to Vivian Bird, the Prince Regent, visiting Ragley Hall (which you will soon see again) at the end of the eighteenth century, suggested to the Marquis that the view from his front door would be enhanced if a 'castle' were to be built on the ridge opposite. The Marquis complied and the folly was built.

When your track angles down to a T-junction, choose the left-hand option and stay on it as it describes an anticlockwise semicircle around the 'castle's' grounds. When the track reaches another junction, again go to the left obtaining, straight ahead, another view of Ragley Hall. As you continue, on clear days good views open out ahead stretching from Bredon to the bowl of hills surrounding the Vale of Evesham.

At the end of the semicircle, the track joins a tarmacked lane which serves the 'castle'. Here you turn right and walk down the lane flanked by flowering trees which, in their season, provide delightful colours. The lane bends sharply right and then gently left and then, as it curves right again, you fork off to a footpath on your left which slants down across two fields. (This path is not waymarked and is easily missed. It lies immediately before a large laburnum tree by which are two gateposts, one wooden and the other of metal.) At the end of the second field, cross a sunken lane and the stile opposite and then go half-left across a large meadow, aiming for a stile in its far left-hand corner. Climb over the stile and then cross the road and turn right to walk through the village of Wixford using an elevated pavement which takes you past picturesque properties.

When you reach the Fish Inn, cross the road and walk through the pub car park. At the end of this, you pass through a wicket gate and proceed through a small caravan park. On emerging into a field, walk straight ahead to a stile. Cross this and swing right to pass a stile on the left and climb gradually past an industrial site and in front of a black-and-white cottage to reach Wixford Church. Turn left up four steps and enter the churchyard passing a thatched shed in which visiting preachers are said to have stabled their horses while they were engaged in the pulpit. Approach the church beneath a mighty yew tree.

It is known that this yew existed in 1669 because, in that year, villagers petitioned the Bishop to overrule the incumbent who wished to cut it down!

You soon reach the shingle-spired church of Saint Milburgha.

Only five churches in this country are dedicated to Saint Milburgha (a name with a variety of spellings), another reference to the name being made on page 31 of this book.

You may well find that, in common with other country churches, the building is locked. Return down the path by which you came and, on your way, see if you can find a coin hidden at the base of the medieval cross in the graveyard. At the bottom of the steps turn sharp left to join a track which slopes up past the east end of the church. You will stay on this nearly-straight bridleway for the best part of a mile, ignoring paths which leave it on either side. You begin by going up a sharp incline and then enjoy the luxury of a long, gentle 'free-wheel' down towards Alcester during which there are good views of Ragley Hall to your left.

The building of Ragley Hall was begun in about 1680 as the seat of the Marquis of Hertford. The east-facing portico, which you can see from here, was added by James Wyatt in about 1800.

As you approach a large roundabout on the busy A46, you pass through a wicket gate and then walk between wooden palings to reach the dual-carriageway. Using the concrete pathways, cross both carriageways with extreme care and then continue ahead soon to swing left alongside an evergreen hedge. At the end of the hedge, turn right through a wicket gate soon to reach a lane onto which you turn right. Walk forward for about 300 yards where you turn left off the lane onto an (easily-missed!) tarmacked path. Cross the River Arrow by a footbridge after which your path curves to the right past a children's playground and between houses and allotments with the tower of Alcester church directly ahead.

Immediately beyond the allotments, go through a kissing gate on the right and, keeping within a few yards of the boundary on your right, continue across the field to pass through (or by) another kissing gate. Walk on beside an elbow of the Arrow to reach, in a few yards, a pair of pollarded willows. Just beyond them, bear slightly left, soon to walk to the left of a hedge to reach and pass through a kissing gate. Now walk between a tall hedge and a metal barrier beside the town's football ground to reach a road. (Here, you might pause to notice, about 75 yards to your right, an ancient, six-arched bridge over the River Arrow which lies downstream from the confluence of the Arrow and the Alne.) Turn left onto the road. At its end, fork left into a cul-de-sac and then use the refuge to cross the road to enter a small park. At the end of this, turn right into Malt Mill Lane which soon swings left.

The refurbishment of this Conservation Area was completed in 1975 and it provides a fascinating array of architectural styles with examples ranging from the fifteenth to the twentieth centuries. The immaculately maintained gardens behind the houses on both sides of the lane are generally open to the public and are well worth inspecting.

At the top of the lane, turn left to reach the church at which you commenced your walk.

18

A Short Excursion into West Warwickshire

This walk, on the extreme western edge of Warwickshire, is almost entirely on field paths.

Distance: 6 miles. (Walkers joining the walk from Arrow should add three-quarters of a mile).
Start: Lay-by on the east side of the B4088 (GR055567).
Maps: Landranger 150; Pathfinder 997; Explorer 205.
Car Parking: Lay-by on the east side of the B4088, 400 yards south of the A422 (GR055567).
Public Transport: Bus service 146 (Birmingham/Evesham) Alight at Arrow village and walk up the A422 (Worcester direction). 100 yards after large roadside notices warning motorists of bends for 1½ miles, join the walk at ★ on page 90. N.B. *This is a busy road with no pavements so please take extreme care.*
Refreshments: Nothing suitable.

FROM the lay-by go through a gate immediately to the north of five-gabled, white-painted houses, this gate bearing contradictory advice in the form of a waymark and a 'Private' notice. Walk on beside the left-hand hedge and, after a few yards, pass through another gate to enter a field. Walk ahead and climb over a stile halfway down the slope. In the next field aim a quarter-left from your original direction, your target stile being a yard or so to the right of a black barn. Beyond the stile, bear left onto a track which leads in front of the barn and eventually reaches a busy road which you cross with care. At the other side of the road are two waymark posts. Select the one on the <u>right</u> and go over a stile beside a gate.

Walk on, ignoring a track which soon leads from a car park into the wood and then keeping the woodland margin close at your left hand. In about half-a-mile and soon after passing a pool, the woodland peters out. Continue, now beside a hedge, for a further 100 yards. After crossing a farm track, go ahead on a thin path and continue down through a large field with, on your right, initially woodland and then a deep ditch and a hedge.

You may well see buzzards while you are on this walk as these large birds of prey are becoming more common in the area. Brown and with rounded wings, their flight, when flushed, is rather laboured. However, once in the air, they soon find thermals on which they soar effortlessly with scarcely any movement of their wings.

At the bottom of this field, veer left for about 20 yards and cross a brick-built bridge and the stile beyond it. Now bear right and, following the boundary, pass through a hedge gap in the right-hand corner of this field. Walk on with a hedge and ditch on your right and, just under 150 yards beyond the next hedge gap, you reach a metal, farm gate on your right. Go through it and walk ahead, close to the hedge on your right, for about 100 yards. At that point, pass over a stile and continue on your former heading, now with the hedge on your left, soon to reach a road. Turn right and walk along the road for 30 yards (the longest road section on the main walk!).

★ *Here, those who have come from the bus stop at Arrow join and leave the walk.*

Turn left through a gateway and follow the field boundary as it gradually curves up towards a disused barn – one of several to be seen from this walk. As you bear left at the barn, Ragley Hall can be seen, amongst trees, to your left.

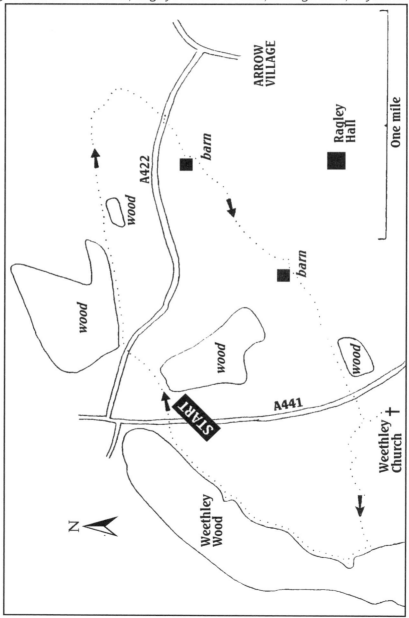

Ragley Hall, built in the late seventeenth century by Robert Hooke, is now owned and occupied by the eighth Marquis of Hertford.

Keeping the field margin on your left, walk on until, at the end of this large field, you cross a stile ahead of you and continue, now with a wire fence on your right. At the end of the wire fence, cross a stile and turn left to continue on your original bearing. At the end of this field, bear right and, in 25 yards, swing left in front of another dilapidated barn. Walk up the stiff slope ahead, crossing a stile beside woodland *en route,* soon to reach a road. Cross the road and walk up the private drive opposite and go through a gate bearing the legend 'Weethley Hamlet'. Extensive views to the west soon open up and, when you have followed the drive as it swings left, you reach the Church of St James, Weethley.

There has been a church on this site since the twelfth century and the pool alongside it is considered to be one of the most natural in the county. You will probably find the church door locked (the reason being the theft from it of its organ) but a seat on the church's south side provides a quiet place to pause, enjoy panoramic views – and, maybe, photograph the gaunt remains of a yew tree against the background of the church.

When you are ready to move on, retrace your steps onto the private drive and, just before this curves off to the right, go through hedge gap on the left and walk straight ahead in the direction of large barns, soon to cross a stile. Now

Weethley Church

walk down the field margin on the left for about 100 yards to reach and cross a stile and walk through a spinney. Leave the spinney by way of a plank bridge and stile and go left onto a cart track

Just before this track appears to split into two, cross a stile on the right and continue down the left-hand side of two fields. After about 200 yards of the second field, look out for a track which goes to the right. (Do not be unduly alarmed if you miss this track. Merely go ahead and, when you reach woodland, turn right along its margin rejoining the main route at a waymark post.) Walk along the track until, at a hedge-end, you will see a path which goes left, passes an isolated ash tree and reaches a waymark-post on the edge of woodland.

If you were to walk ahead into Weethley Wood for about 200 yards, you would cross the county boundary into Worcestershire and, about a mile ahead, reach the delightful village of Abbots Morton which was visited on Walk 17 of More Country Walks.

At the waymark post, turn right and follow the meandering woodland margin for about a mile – but never entering the woodland.

As you go, look out for fallow deer which, having come out to graze on nearby crops, will dash back to the sanctuary of the trees. In summer, you may also see, at your feet, the flowers of scarlet pimpernel, also known as the Poor Man's Weatherglass.

At one stage, you are obliged to make a sharp left turn, by a woodworm-ridden oak, to go through a hedge gap and, a little over a quarter of a mile beyond this, you reach a gate marked 'Private. Please Keep Out'. Here turn right and walk away from the wood on a rough track, soon to reach the road and your starting place.

If you joined the walk near Arrow continue by following the instructions from the beginning.

19

Harvington and some of the Lench Villages

'Lench' means 'hill' so this walk through some of the Lench villages is best done on a clear day when attractive views may be on offer and/or at 'blossom time'. The prefixes, Atch, Rous, etc. refer to medieval manorial possessions.

Distance: 8½ miles.
Start: Harvington (near Evesham), The Coach and Horses in Church Street (GR057489).
Maps: Landranger 150; Pathfinder 1020 & 997; Explorer 205.
Car Parking: The Coach and Horses in Harvington – *but please ask the publican's permission first.*
Public Transport: Bus services 28/29 (also 166, Suns & bank holidays only) between Evesham and Stratford. Alight at the Coach and Horses, Harvington (not the Golden Cross).
Refreshments: The Coach and Horses – of course!

FROM The Coach and Horses, turn right into Church Street, soon passing St James' church (surrounded in early spring by colourful crocuses, daffodils and snowdrops) and delightful cottages.

As Church Street swings left, turn right into an un-named road soon passing 'The Retreat' and a giant horse chestnut. 80 yards beyond this tree, turn left into Grange Lane at the top of which your right of way joins a private drive. After a further 40 yards, you bear left and then right to join a footpath onto which you bear right. After walking initially between paddock railings on your left and a beech hedge on your right, stay on this clear path until you reach a road. Here turn left and walk to the crossroads at which you turn right to walk beside the B4088. After about 120 yards, join a footpath on the left.

Wind your way along this well-used track, bearing slightly left after passing a ruined cottage on your left (which may be in the process of redevelopment or demolition) and farm buildings on your right. *Be alert here* for, about 70 yards after the cottage, you leave the track to begin your gradual ascent up to Atch Lench. Going a quarter-right from the track (on an *easily-missed* path), aim for the near end of a hedge some 600 yards ahead, 50 yards or so to the left of an electricity pylon. On reaching this hawthorn hedge (hopefully, it will not be removed in the process of 'prairie-isation' which seems to be rife hereabouts), walk along a tractor track on its right. When you reach the end of the hedge, continue on the track until, very soon after it bends to the left, you turn onto a footpath on your right, resuming your original heading. On reaching a line of trees, cross a brook and veer left and, soon afterwards, right to continue your climb to the right of another hedge.

At the end of this hedge, again perform a quick left-right manoeuvre and continue upwards, the gradient soon steepening noticeably. Here, you are but a couple of hundred yards to the west of the Warwickshire border. When you reach the top of the slope, you may wish – if you haven't done so already – to pause and look back at the fine panorama which will be on view on clear days. The ridge of hills stretches from Oversley Castle on the left (seen on Walk 17) round to Bredon on the right

Having regained your breath, bear left onto a clear bridleway, possibly seeing, to the left of a black-and-white thatched cottage, a distant glimpse of the Malverns. Bear left to walk in front of houses and turn right onto the lane by the

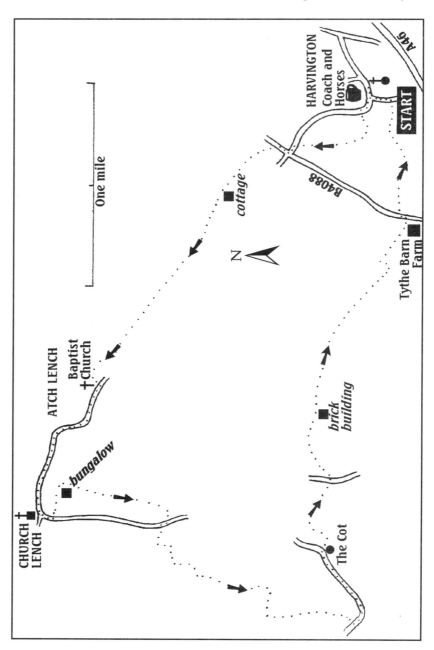

thatched cottage. Having passed the Atch Lench Baptist Chapel and more thatched cottages, stay on this road as it snakes its way down and up to the next village, Church Lench. All Saints' Church lies at the top of the hill.

The absence of public houses in the Lench villages is attributed to Rev. William Kyle Westwood Chafy-Chafy who was squire and parson at Rous Lench in the 1870s and was, to quote Vivian Bird, 'an opponent of beer and Baptists'. He was also responsible for the various biblical references, under the heading 'Laus Deo', which are carved into the stonework of Church Lench Church of England First School (opposite the church) – and for others that you will see later.

Immediately beyond the church, turn left onto Evesham Road. After about 80 yards, and just before a garden commemorating the Silver Jubilee of 1977, turn left onto a tarmac path. After about 20 yards, go through a metal, wicket gate on your left and continue on an enclosed path. After passing by (but <u>not</u> through) a old wooden kissing-gate, walk ahead with the field boundary on your left. On reaching a bridleway by a red-roofed bungalow, turn right and go ahead for after about half-a-mile, crossing two stiles and passing a fishing pool, conifers and an orchard *en route*. When you reach a workshop, turn right and walk ahead to meet a road onto which you turn right. After just less that 100 yards, cross a stile on the left.

You are still on the Wychavon Way, a 40-mile long-distance path connecting Holt Fleet, on the River Severn, and Winchcombe in the Cotswolds. A public footpath is 'a highway over which the right of way is on foot only' i.e. footpaths are reserved for humans. You may find that, for the next mile or so, this one has been used by horse-riders with consequent damage to its surface.

Follow the hedge on your right as it makes four ninety-degree turns. After the fourth, continue down a slope, cross a footbridge and turn left. Now walk on with the hedge on your left as it twists up a slope for about 700 yards where, near the top of the slope, a cart track goes off to the right.

On reaching this cart track, pause to look at you next objective – the farm and group of houses a quarter-left ahead. However, you will see that the direct route is not available to you, the footpath having been diverted 'by statutory order'.

So turn right and walk down the track and, at the bottom, turn left to walk with a stream deep down on your right. After about 300 yards, go through a hedge gap on your right and then immediately pass through another on your left, to resume your former bearing, now to the right of the stream. On reaching a road, turn left and follow it, soon bearing left and bidding farewell to the Wychavon Way. Walk on to the village of Sheriff's Lench. Soon after entering the village, turn right into a lane, passing to the left of an elaborately-chimneyed, black-and-white house, 'The Cot', built in 1871.

This house bears the inscriptions: 'The time is short' and 'Here have we no continuing city but we seek one to come' – again showing the influence of Chafy-Chafy. The house on the other side of the lane bears his initials, WKWCC.

In about 70 yards, just beyond more houses, bear slightly left and, on reaching the first electricity post, bear left again to walk along the edge of an orchard – the first of several which you will see on your walk back to

Harvington. Continue beyond the third post for 10 yards and then turn right to walk beside an overgrown hedge until you reach a road. (The cottages on your right also bear the WKWCC motif.)

You are faced with metal railings. A few yards to your right look for an unobtrusive wooden step by which you can get over these railings. Having negotiated this barrier, the line of your path now follows the row of trees in front of you, this having once marked a field boundary. After the last (seventh) tree, veer slightly right to an isolated, ivy-clad ash tree and then onwards to a hedge elbow. Having reached this, continue for about 30 yards when you turn right to walk across the field to pass through a muddy hedge gap. Now walk straight up to the top of the ridge aiming just left of a flat-topped brick building.

This concrete-topped, brick-walled building is filled with brick rubble. A similar, less robust, building is to be seen a few hundred yards further along the ridge. Despite enquiries, the writer has been unable to find out their history. Could they have been World War II gun emplacements or searchlight batteries?

From this building, go a quarter-left across the next field, your bearing being a few degrees to the left of the top of an electricity pylon. On reaching your target – a bramble-lined hedge gap – go through it and then walk straight down the next field, hopefully enjoying – again the fine panorama that you saw from Atch Lench earlier.

Until it was cleared by Czech workers during World War II in order to increase agricultural capacity, this slope (called Rough Hills) was tree-covered.

As the slope eases, continue ahead on a broad, grassy path between arable fields, the one on your right being the longer one. Maybe you will notice the square tower of Norton church to your half-right. At the end of the right-hand field, go ahead, now with a hedge on your left and a bramble thicket on your right. You soon walk beside a windbreak hedge between well-groomed orchards and, after nearly 300 yards, you reach a stout electricity pole. Here you turn left and, in 60 yards, bear right to walk beside another windbreak hedge.

These windbreaks are important in minimising the damage done by late frosts to fruit trees in blossom. Such late frosts can devastate subsequent crops. (Some of these hedges are, apparently, scheduled for removal.)

Walk to the left of the buildings of Tythe Barn Farm soon to reach the busy B4088 onto which you turn left. In just under 60 yards, cross the road and join a broad path between a bungalow and a house. Continue between further orchards and, at the end of another long windbreak, turn right to follow a barbed wire fence with which you make three right-angle turns before continuing down a slope to a footbridge. Beyond this, an enclosed path leads up to houses where it turns right. Follow its meanderings until it broadens and leads down to a road into which you turn left.

The large tree on the corner is a Holm Oak – hence the name of the house in the garden of which it stands. Introduced from the Mediterranean area early in the sixteenth century for its ornamental rather than its commercial value, the young leaves of this evergreen tree are often spiny – hence its other name 'Holly Oak'.

Continue up the road, soon bearing right and, passing the church, you reach the starting point.

20

Brideshead Visited

Distance: 9½ miles.
Start: This depends on your mode of travel. The main start is at a drinking fountain (GR 782474) and applies if you are coming from Great Malvern, are using a bus that goes past Malvern Link station on the A449, or are arriving by train at Malvern Link station. Carefully cross the A449 to the drinking fountain.
For car travellers, on leaving the car park, join Pickersleigh Avenue, turn left and, in 120 yards, turn left into a road signposted to the business park and rugby club, joining the walk at ★ below.
Maps: Landranger 150; Explorer 14.
Car Parking: There is a free car park in Pickersleigh Avenue, 130 yards from its intersection with the A449 in Malvern Link. (If full, use adjacent roadsides.)
Public Transport: Trains and buses to Malvern Link or Great Malvern.
Refreshments: Abundant facilities in Malvern Link and in Great Malvern town.
! At the time of writing, the construction of the business park near the start of this walk was incomplete and footpaths through it were disrupted. Therefore, to avoid confusion, the route uses roads through this area.

THE main start is at the drinking fountain (GR 782474) erected, in 1900, by the British Women's Temperance Association. This is prominent on the Worcester Road (A449) a few yards on the Malvern town side of the railway bridge adjacent to Malvern Link station. Walk down the road, away from the Malvern Hills, very soon to cross the railway bridge and reach the common on the right-hand side of the road.

Bear half-right across the common, passing through the left-hand edge of a spinney and aiming towards a sharply-gabled house with white, metal balconies. To the left of this, and beside Link End Lodge, take an enclosed path. At the end of this, you cross a road and enter a similar path opposite you. When you come to another road, cross it, go slightly right and walk down another road signposted to a business park and rugby club.

★ *Car travellers join here.*

At the next road junction, go right and walk on past industrial units. Just before the end of this road, turn right into Spring Lane South and, when you reach a mini-roundabout, turn left into Sandy's Road. At the next roundabout, turn left (onto the B4208) and continue for a little over 150 yards. When you reach lamppost number 41, cross the road and walk ahead onto a fenced-off path which leads between newly-planted trees, soon to cross a stile. Proceed straight ahead to climb over another stile beyond which you cross a paddock. Go forward to negotiate a further stile, cross a lane and join the path opposite which leads, just to the right of a small stream, along the edge of a patch of woodland. At the end of this, go over a stile, turn left and walk along the edge of a long pool well-stocked with bulrushes.

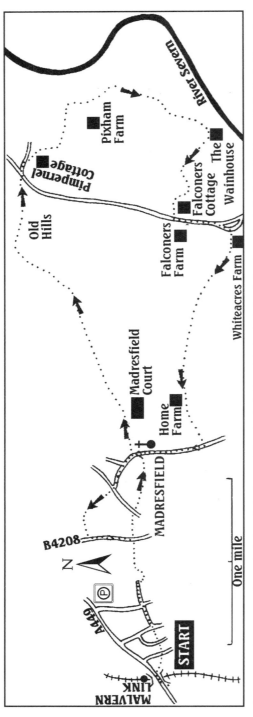

Though more correctly called 'reedmace', the name 'bulrush' is now commonly applied to this plant. Its familiar brown, sausage-shaped seed heads are formed in the summer but the seeds are not shed until early the following year.

Beyond the pool, a pair of stiles separated by a muddy field-end must be crossed before you pass up a slight incline on a wide farm-track with the spire of Madresfield church initially directly ahead. At the end of the track, pass over the stile in the right-hand corner and then bear quarter-left to a stile some 30 yards to the left of red-brick cottages. Cross the stile and pass through the metal gate beyond it to reach a road. At the other side of the road, turn left. In about 100 yards, immediately after passing a picturesque lodge with an extravagant chimney, turn right onto a tarmacked lane, the large variety of mature trees on your right hiding Madresfield Court which you will see later.

When the lane forks, bear right and continue, soon to walk beneath a couple of brick bridges. 40 yards beyond the second bridge, the lane swings right. On this bend, look out for a metal kissing-gate on the left. Pass through this and, veering very slightly left, gradually come to and follow this large field's left-hand boundary which is adjacent to the tree-shrouded Madresfield Brook which you will cross later. After about 500 yards, cross a stile at the end of the field and bear left, continuing to follow the next field's meandering margin for a further half-mile.

When you reach a metal, farm gate on the left, pass through it and cross a brick bridge. Veer slightly right until, in the far corner of the field, you see two farm gates. Cross the stile alongside the one on your right and in less than 10 yards, climb over another stile on your left to enter a wood. Walk on a clear path through bracken, going ahead at a cross-path, soon to leave the woodland via another stile. Walk straight across the next field to cross a pair of stiles beneath a nearly-dead oak. Now turn right soon to pass through a wicket gate. Walk straight forward through a rather boggy area with no clear path but very soon start a gradual ascent of the grassy slope of Old Hills.

The name Old Hills is thought to be a corruption of Wold Hills, suggesting complete tree-cover. This area is under the benevolent supervision of the Malvern Hills Conservators, a body which was set up by Act of Parliament in 1884 and which has done much good work in the area of the Malverns and their surroundings.

Having passed the trig point at the brow of the hill, walk straight down the other side enjoying this viewpoint (with Worcester and its Cathedral over to your left). Soon pass a white house on the left and join a rough driveway to pass more houses. When this driveway swings off abruptly to the right, walk ahead on grass aiming for a red, mail box. Just beyond this, cross the road with great care (this is a dangerous bend!) and go ahead onto a lane signposted 'Pixham'. A few yards before the second electricity post, take a grassy path which slants up to your right, following the left-hand option when it very soon forks. Continue to ascend and when you reach the thatched Pimpernel Cottage bear left and then right, following its boundary to pass over a stile behind the house. Here you enter a wedge-shaped strip of meadowland. Follow the electricity wires for 150 yards or so and, at the second electricity post, cross the stile on your left and go straight ahead over a long mound.

N.B. At the time of writing it was not possible at this point to follow the right of way as shown on the O.S. Map. However, the route described is well used.

Despite your proximity to the Severn, your only sight of the river (unless it is in flood) will be slightly to your right as you cross the mound. A little further to your right, on the horizon, is Bredon Hill which is visited on Walk 21 in this book. The black-and-white residence which you can see about 500 yards half-left is Pixham House. Near this, an old ferry, long-since gone, was used by Simon de Montford to take his troops across the river to the ill-fated Battle of Evesham. Beyond Pixham House, on the other side of the river, Kempsey church is to be seen.

Having descended from the mound and reached the end of the field, pass through a gate, cross a farm drive and bear right to walk with a hedge (and, for a short distance, a wire fence) on your left.

Go through a gate ahead of you (not the one on your left) and follow the now-more-distinct bridleway, soon to pass beneath pylon-borne, electricity supply cables. Stay on the bridleway until, having passed through another gate and come abreast of a patch of thick woodland on your right, you go slightly right across the field to pass through a gateway to the left of a pylon which stands close to a flood defence barrier. Soon bear right over the barrier, pass through a metal gate and go over Madresfield Brook by way of a moss-covered bridge. Now follow the left-hand boundary as you walk up a sharp slope.

When you reach the top of the slope, bear right across the field on a grassy path, the imposing Malvern ridge now coming into full view. Now follow a fence and an intermittent hedge on your right until, just before The Wainhouse, one of the converted buildings of Clevelode Farm, you turn sharply right onto another bridleway which leads past a pylon. Follow this track for about 500 yards and, a few paces after crossing a stream (Whiteacres Brook), go left through a hedge gap. Your path leads straight across the next field where you pass through another hedge gap and turn right to walk up a slope towards a pair of houses. After the next stile, you walk ahead across the lawn in front of the house on the right (Falconers Cottage), soon to veer left onto a track which leads, in front of the other house, towards a busy road.

When you reach the road, cross it, turn left and walk on with great care until, 300 yards past Falconers Farm, you fork right onto an old road (soon noticing an old milestone on your left). Immediately beyond Whiteacres Cottage (yellow-walled and built in 1865), turn right and, just before the brick gate-posts of Whiteacres Farm, again turn right to cross a stile which is partly hidden by a twin-trunked ash tree. Now proceed with wooden palings at you left hand to reach and cross another stile beyond which you go right and follow the field boundary. At the top of the ridge, the hedge ends. Walk on for 15 yards. At that point, you need to go two-thirds left to reach a wicket gate at a hedge elbow. However, crops may prevent this and oblige you to go left and then right to reach this gate. Having passed through it, go diagonally left across the next field aiming for a gateway in the far left-hand corner and which is almost in line with the magnificent Madresfield Court. Go through the gateway and follow a farm track as it passes through two further gates, veers right and then left and leads towards the black-and-white gable end of Home Farm.

Madresfield Court, for centuries the home of the Lygons, is where parts of the television spectacular, Brideshead Revisited *were filmed.*

As you approach the farm, you will notice what looks like a sail-less windmill but is, in fact, a well-maintained dovecote with twenty-four holes above which is a large 'B', the whole surmounted by an elaborate weathervane. (Presumably the 'B' stands for the Beauchamp family, which married into the Lygon family in the 1700s. The same cipher is to be seen later on some of the houses in the village.) Walk on through the farmyard, pass houses and veer left down an avenue, mainly of limes, at the end of which, beyond two venerable oaks and another splendid lodge, you reach a road. Here turn right (using a wide grass verge which is particularly useful when the road sweeps to the right) and walk on to the church.

The church of St Mary the Virgin, Madresfield, which was built in the middle 1860s, sports a pinnacled spire and, near its south door, has an unusual well-head, set on steps and surmounted by a wrought iron canopy.

On leaving via the lychgate, turn right and, after re-walking a small section of your outward route, follow the road as it swings left and then continue straight ahead when the main road soon veers right again. At a T-junction, cross the road and go over a stile at the side of the gate ahead of you. After about 60 yards, the field margin swings away to the left. Here go half-right across the field, in the direction of a church spire peeping over tree tops. On reaching the other side of the field, go through a gap and then immediately turn left.

When the Safeway supermarket comes into view, you soon come to a gateway on your left. Do not pass through this but, 45 yards beyond it, leave the main path, veer slightly left to cross a stile and soon swing left between the hedge and an area of young saplings. When you reach a road (the B4208 again), cross it and turn left. At the first roundabout, turn right into Grovewood Road and, at the next, go left into Betony Road. At the end of Betony Road, you rejoin your outward route by turning right in Sandy's Road and, from it, turning right into Spring Lane South. At the end of this, turn left to walk up the road between the industrial units. Fork left by a white house, pass the entrance to the rugby ground and walk up to a T-junction.

Here, the two routes separate. For the car park turn right and walk along Pickersleigh Avenue. For Malvern Link station, etc. bear slightly right across the road to enter the enclosed path, continuing on this after crossing another road. Beyond the next road, bear half-right to walk across parkland to the railway bridge.

21

Pershore, Bredon Hill and some of the 'Bredon Villages'

If you are lucky with the weather and you choose the right season, you might well share A.E.Housman's feelings about 'summertime on Bredon' where he admired 'the coloured counties' and heard 'the larks so high about us in the sky'.

Distance: Longer route (starting from Pershore Bridges) 14 miles. Shorter route (starting from Little Comberton) 9½ miles.
Start: Longer walk: Pershore Bridges Picnic Place (GR952451) which is just south of the Avon alongside the A44 road from Pershore to Evesham. Shorter walk: Top of Manor Lane, Little Comberton. Start reading from ★ on page 107
Maps: Landranger 150; Explorer 14.
Car Parking: There is limited parking at the Pershore Bridges Picnic Place where the walk starts (GR952452). Otherwise in Pershore. Note: Those who are looking for a shorter walk and who have their own transport may wish to start and finish at the Village Hall on the main road through Little Comberton (GR967429). (There is a small car park there, though it may be full when events are taking place at the Hall. Otherwise, suitable parking spaces will be found on side roads in the village.) From the Village Hall turn left and in 100 yards or so pass the end of Manor Lane, joining the walk at ★ on page 104.
Public Transport: Bus service 551/557 (Worcester/Evesham) stopping at Pershore. Using service 551, from the Broad Street stop walk along Bridge Street to reach the start of the main walk. Service 557 (less regular) will drop you at the start.
For the shorter walk, bus service 392 (Pershore/Evesham) stopping at Great Comberton (limited service). Also 565 from Pershore to Great Comberton (very limited).
Refreshments: There are plenty of facilities in Pershore but the only pubs *en route* are The Queen's and the Old Mill in Elmley Castle.

The Pershore Bridges starting point is an interesting spot between the old and the new bridges but do not tarry too long as you have a hard day ahead of you, this being by far the most demanding walk in the book.

Use the underpass to walk beneath the road to emerge again at the edge of the River Avon, making its leisurely way from Naseby to Tewkesbury, 58 of its 96 miles being in Warwickshire. It must have looked far from tranquil in early April 1998 when three inches of rain fell here in twenty-four hours! Turn left just beyond the information board and walk alongside the A44, soon passing the site of a World War II gun emplacement. Reaching a side-road, turn right and proceed on the nearside pavement for 150 yards to the road junction where you continue straight ahead. After another 500 yards, immediately after house no. 17 on the left, fork left onto an unnamed, rougher road with Great Comberton church and Bredon Tower now in view ahead of you, each of which you will visit later.

On reaching a house sheltered by tall evergreens, the tarmac gives way to shale. Your path goes ahead, ruler-straight, between horticultural crops for about 600 yards, the second section of it (after the shale track swings right) running to the left of a poplar hedge after which it becomes a grassy path which ends at the charmingly named Mary Brook. Here turn right and walk beside the brook for a little more than 100 yards to reach a footbridge. Cross this, and the stile at the other side, and then turn right.

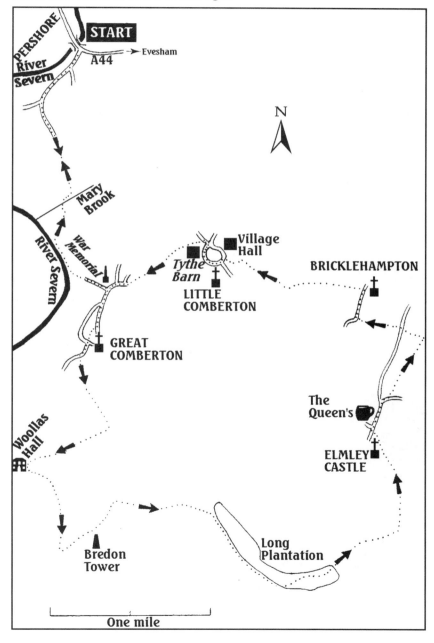

After 40 yards, you come to a hedge. Here turn left and walk up a slope with the hedge on your right. Near the top of the incline follow the hedge as it swings right past a little group of willows. Climb over two stiles in the corner and continue along the right hand margin of a large field which may, in summer, have caravans parked in it. At the far end, cross the first stile, ignore the second and slant left down towards the river. Turn left to follow the riverbank, crossing a stile beside a gate and skirting a golf course at the end of which a stile leads you into a wooded area. In 10 yards fork left and follow the ascending path soon to reach a lane (Quay Lane) onto which you bear left and continue upwards to the T-junction near the War Memorial.

★ ★ *The shorter route joins here.*

Here, turn right and, after a couple of hundred yards, fork left into Church Street. Walk on to enter the graveyard of St Michael's Church.

This is the first of four churches that you pass on this walk, approaching it beneath the branches of an ancient yew tree which has a girth of over 17 feet.

Standing with your back to the church door (which is at the west end), take a path to your left which goes to the right of the black-and-white Church Cottage. Pass through a metal kissing gate and follow an enclosed path soon to emerge at a T-junction where you walk down the road straight ahead of you, signposted Eckington and Bredon. At the bottom of a sharp incline, the road swings right. Here go left over a stile beneath an old willow and follow the

Great Comberton Church

hedge as you begin your two-stage ascent of Bredon Hill. When you need to pause for breath, look back at the good views north over Worcestershire with the magnificent Malvern ridge to the west. After crossing a stile continue forward with the field boundary still on the left, then at the next stile, walk to the right keeping just up-hill from the wire fence.

For the next couple of miles of this walk, you may be fortunate enough to surprise one or more fallow deer. The sandy-coloured flanks of these deer are decorated with white spots and the tail is black with white undersides.

Your next objective is not immediately apparent

but keep going and you will find that the wire fence eventually comes back into view as it curves round to reach a stile and a farm gate.

Cross the stile, continue forward, and soon come to a Malverns-facing seat beside a plaque which commemorates tree planting in 1992. Continue on this fairly level track (ignoring a track turning off on the right that leads to Woollas Hall Farm) until you reach Woollas Hall.

The first record of a house on the site of Woollas Hall was in 1219, the current building dating from 1611. Now divided into flats, the house apparently still retains some of its fine features, including a magnificent Jacobean staircase.

Having walked between the Coach House and the main building and admired well-maintained gardens, retrace your steps and, 10 yards beyond the cattle grid, with Pershore Abbey visible straight ahead, cross the stile on your right. You now start the second part of your ascent of Bredon Hill. Now veering a little to your left and having kept to the left of a reedy stream, at the top corner of the field you reach a farm gate with adjoining cattle grid. Beyond this gate, walk up a stony track. In about 130 yards, leave the track, fork right and cross a stile.

Now veer two-thirds-left up the grassy slope. Aim for a stile at the top right-hand corner of the field, some 250 yards to the right of communication discs. Beyond this stile, your path continues in a gully which meanders up to the plateau. In summer you may notice numerous butterflies which are attracted to the nectar-rich thistles which are abundant hereabouts. Cross an interesting gate-stile and at the top, having become aware of fresh views which have opened up ahead of you, turn left onto a bridleway, pass through a farm gate at the end of a copse and bear left to follow the wall to reach and enjoy one of south Worcestershire's finest viewpoints.

The exact date at which Bredon Tower was built is open to debate but it seems certain that William Parsons of Kemerton (one of the 'Bredon Villages') constructed it as a summer house sometime in the eighteenth century. The height of the hill is 961 feet and it is suggested that 'Parson's Folly', which measures 39 feet, was built to take the height of the hill to the magic 1000 feet mark. Prior to World War II, the folly was said to house a hermit, but it served as an RAF observation post during that war and it now acts as a relay station for a mobile phone company.

Walk on with the wall on your left (ignoring a wicket gate and a stone stile in this wall) until you go through a gate to the left of a wooded area. Here you lose the wall but continue in the same direction, soon with a wire fence at your right hand. Continue on the bridleway beyond the next gate, the marvellous views now having become obscured by the thick woodland of Long Plantation.

This bridleway is flanked by many burdock plants, the seed heads of which are equipped with sharply-hooked 'burs' which, by becoming attached to the fur of passing mammals (or to the clothing of passing ramblers), assist the plants' dispersal. Reputedly, these devices were the inspiration of the inventor of Velcro fasteners.

Leave behind another communications tower on your right: on reaching a farm gate on the right the path widens out significantly. Here fork left following the blue waymarks of the Wychavon Way which slants down through the woodland. Leaving this behind at a wicket gate, you then proceed through

rough pasture towards the village of Elmley Castle, your direction being indicated at intervals by waymark posts (or by following the abundant hoof-prints of the horses which share your path). However, you should ignore signs which show black arrows on white backgrounds as these direct riders taking part in horse trials which cross your path.

After crossing a bridge, bear half-left and continue down the grassy surface. Cross another footbridge and swing left, soon passing the end of an L-shaped pool. Immediately after passing through a wooden wicket gate, turn left, cross a footbridge and stile and then go three-quarters-right, passing to the right of an ailing oak and a healthier horse chestnut. On crossing a stile and footbridge in the hedge at the field's end, go half-left, aiming for a stile 50 yards to the left of a green-roofed shed. Cross this dog-friendly stile and use a short, well-trodden path to reach woodland. Here, climb over a stile and bear right to walk past (and, maybe, rest awhile beside) fishponds before entering the churchyard of St Mary's, Elmley Castle.

This is the second church on your circuit. It has old oak pews and stone-flagged aisles and, amongst its interesting features, its thirteenth century font has four dragons writhing at its base.

Leaving the church, walk past an imposing sundial and go through the gate at the churchyard's north end, soon pass The Queen's, a pub so named to commemorate the visit to the village of Queen Elizabeth I on August 20 1575. Continue straight down the broad, main street with its sunken stream beside you. Just beyond the village school, fork right onto the road to Netherton passing an ancient pillar (old market cross?) at the road junction.

In 50 yards or so, just beyond a converted barn called The Long House, pass through a wicket gate on your left. This path is initially enclosed but, when it emerges into fields, ignore a stile on the left and stay on the same bearing, with the boundary on your left. Continue until you reach an isolated, multi-trunked willow. Cross the plank bridge immediately beyond this and walk across the next field to reach a road in front of a red-brick and white-painted house. Turn right onto the road and, in 20 yards, turn left onto a bridleway, initially with a tall evergreen hedge at your left hand. Continue ahead to join tarmac and, when you reach the next road, turn right and walk into the tiny village of Bricklehampton.

About 50 yards beyond the church's lych-gate, take a footpath on your left which crosses a paddock, passing to the right of twin electricity posts. At the far side, duck under the railings, cross a stile and proceed with the hedge on your right through two fields (ignoring a path left on entering the second field), the church tower of Little Comberton coming into view after a few score yards, backed by the Malverns. After going under triple electricity cables, follow the hedge as it goes left and right and cross a stile in the field's corner. In order to reach the far hedgerow, you go left and follow the hedge, walking round a close hairpin bend. Ignore a stile on the hairpin and, about 220 yards after more overhead wires, you reach the end of the field.

Here turn left and, in about 20 yards pass a footbridge on the right but then, a yard or so further on, cross a stile and plank bridge also on your right. Walk on, with the hedge on your right, and, at the end of the field, swing left and, in just less than 100 yards, pass through a pair of wicket gates on your right. Walk beneath the spreading boughs of a lime tree and continue straight across an orchard to reach a kissing gate by a large silver birch. Some steps lead you down to a road where you turn left soon to walk beneath a huge cedar tree as you enter the churchyard of St Peter's Church, Little Comberton.

The informative church leaflet welcomes you 'to our Parish Church, nestling in the shadow of Bredon Hill, where the people of Little Comberton have worshipped for 800 years'. In the south-west corner of the churchyard is the grave of Edward Charles Harris who died in 1982. The lower end of the cross carved on the tombstone is fashioned into a four-pronged garden fork which, maybe, reflected the wide range of Mr Harris's former duties as churchwarden.

Leave the churchyard and turn left into Manor Lane which soon loops right, passing interesting thatched houses and an old Tythe Barn. When it rejoins the busy main road, you turn left.

★ *The shorter walk starts and ends here.*

In 50 yards or so take a footpath on your left immediately before a house called 'The Nest'. After a stile, go half-right across pronounced ridge-and-furrow (which changes direction halfway across the field), targeting a footbridge in the far corner. Beyond this, go straight across the next field, your path following the line of electricity poles. At the far side, go over a plank bridge beside one of the poles. At the next pole, go slightly left to another footbridge. Having crossed this, go half-left to the far corner of the field where a hedge-gap leads to a road which leads to Great Comberton's War Memorial, a short distance beyond which you come to Quay Lane.

Those following the shorter route walk ahead and continue from ★ ★ *on page 104*

Those who are retracing their steps to Pershore turn right here and walk down Quay Lane. A few paces beyond Quay Cottage, bear slightly right onto a woodland path. Just before that path reaches the Avon, turn right, cross a stile and walk along the riverbank to cross a stile beside a gate. At the end of a further strip of riverside grassland, bear right, walk up the slope to find and cross the right-hand one of a pair of stiles in the corner.

Walk ahead, the hedge on your left and, at the end of the field, cross a pair of stiles. Now follow the hedge soon to veer left and walk down towards Mary Brook. Here, turn right, for a few paces where you cross the footbridge that you negotiated earlier in the day. Turn right, walk for 100 yards and then turn left onto the grassy strip, pass the poplar hedge, walk along the gravel track, pass the evergreen-sheltered house and join the roughly tarmacked lane. Turn right at the next road junction, go straight ahead at the next, and, just before the main road, turn left past the gun emplacement and return through the underpass to your starting point by the Avon.

Index

Also by Des Wright…

COUNTRY WALKS IN WARWICKSHIRE AND WORCESTERSHIRE

Twenty circular walks in two fine counties from a popular author whose love of the countryside is abundantly evident in this book. The walks explore some of the counties' most attractive areas, with easy walking, mostly on the flat and with few climbs. Distances range from 2½ to 8½ miles although some can be combined to give longer walks.

ISBN 1 869922 33 6. £5.95. 96 pages. 16 photographs. 21 maps.

MORE COUNTRY WALKS IN WARWICKSHIRE AND WORCESTERSHIRE

A second collection of circular walks. As in the first collection the walking is not difficult with few climbs. Distances range from 4½ to 11½ miles, with most walks having a shorter option of between 1½ and 8 miles. All are readily accessible by car and by public transport.

ISBN 1 869922 37 9. £5.95. 112 pages. 22 photographs. 20 maps.

Also from Meridian…

WALKS IN SOUTH WARWICKSHIRE
From Shakespeare Country to the Cotswolds

by John W Parnham and Barry R Wills

This collection of circular walks represent the authors' favourites within this lovely, varied region. The walks will take you along ancient trackways and paths, past standing stones, earthworks, country estates and grand houses. In the Arden countryside as well as finding connections to William Shakespeare you will discover hidden valleys and distinct wooded hilltops that offer wonderful views. Further south the walks will take you through delightful villages and into remote areas in the Cotswold Hills that rival in many ways the better known parts of this beautiful region.

ISBN 1 869922 38 7. Price £6.95. 112 pages. 36 sketches. 18 maps.

WALKS AROUND THE MALVERNS
by Roy Woodcock

The Malvern Hills and their surroundings provide magnificent opportunities for rambling, and in this book of twenty walks Roy Woodcock explores many of their superb features. The walks cover the entire range of hills and the

neighbouring commons, together with some of the delightful countryside nearby. Distances range from two miles to eight miles, plus a leg stretcher of between ten and sixteen miles (depending on the starting point) that takes in the full length of the ridge and ascends all the Malvern peaks.
ISBN 1 869922 32 8. £6.95. 112 pages. 32 illustrations. 20 maps.

THE NAVIGATION WAY
A Hundred Mile Towpath Walk

by Peter Groves and Trevor Antill

Starting from the centre of Birmingham and encompassing fourteen West Midlands canals the Navigation Way follows a meandering course through varied urban areas and delightful countryside until terminating at Chasewater. Now again revised to cover the many changes and improvements that have been made to the towpaths its twelve sections provide a series of walks ranging from 5¼ to 11 miles. The book also contains ten additional circular 'canal-link' walks in some of the attractive walking areas adjacent to the canals.
Third revised edition. ISBN 1 869922 35 2. £5.95. 112 pages. 34 photographs. 24 maps.

WATERSIDE WALKS IN THE MIDLANDS

by Birmingham Ramblers: edited by Peter Groves

Twenty-two walks featuring brooks, streams, pools, rivers and canals. Some can be found a short distance from the centre of Britain's second city; others will take the reader further afield in the West Midlands and into the attractive counties of Warwickshire, Worcestershire, Shropshire, Staffordshire and Derbyshire.
ISBN 1 869922 09 3. £4.95. 112 pages. 28 photographs. 22 maps.

MORE WATERSIDE WALKS IN THE MIDLANDS

by Birmingham Ramblers: edited by Peter Groves

A second collection of walks featuring brooks, streams, rivers, canals and pools – sometimes as a major aspect of a walk, sometimes as a feature to encounter as you ramble through some of the fine Midlands countryside.
ISBN 1 869922 31 X. £5.95 112 pages. 21 photographs. 18 maps. Paperback. A5.

FAVOURITE WALKS IN THE WEST MIDLANDS

by members of the Birmingham CHA Rambling Club, Edited
by Tom Birch and Mary Wall
A collection of twenty-two attractive walks from members of one of
Birmingham's oldest walking clubs.
ISBN 1 869922 26 3. £4.95. 112 pages. 24 photographs. 23 maps.

THE ELAN VALLEY WAY

by David Milton
The Elan Valley Way runs from Frankley, on the western fringe of
Birmingham, to the Elan Valley in mid-Wales. Largely following footpaths
and bridleways, and with many superb views, the 128½ mile route passes
through some delightful walking areas in the counties of Worcestershire,
Shropshire, Herefordshire and Powys.
ISBN 1 869922 39 5. Price £7.95. 160 pages. 21 photographs. 21 maps.

Available from booksellers or, if in difficulty, direct from the
publishers.

Please send your remittance, including the following amounts for
postage and packing:
Order value up to £10.00 add £1.00;
over £10.00 and up to £20.00 add £2.00;
over £20.00 add £2.50.

Meridian Books
40 Hadzor Road Oldbury West Midlands B68 9LA
Tel: 0121-429 4397

Please send for our complete catalogue